GW00986509

Year of tł

A Spirituality for Lovers

DANIEL J. O'LEARY

PAULIST PRESS
New York · Mahwah

The Publisher gratefully acknowledges the use of selected excerpts from: *The Passionate Life* by Sam Keen, copyright © 1983 by Sam Keen, reprinted by permission of Harper & Row, Publishers, Inc.; *The Seven Mysteries of Life* by Guy Murchie, copyright © 1978 by Guy Murchie, reprinted by permission of Houghton Mifflin Company; *The Universe is a Green Dragon: A Cosmic Creation Story* by Brian Swimme and *To Care for the Earth: A Call to a New Theology* by Sean McDonagh, used by permission of Bear & Company Publishing.

Book design by *Nighthawk Design*.

Library of Congress Cataloging-in-Publication Data

O'Leary, Daniel J.
Year of the heart : a spirituality for lovers / Daniel J. O'Leary.
p.   cm.
Bibliography: p.
ISBN 0-8091-3081-5 : $6.95 (est.)
1. Spiritual life—Catholic authors.   I. Title.
BX2350.2.04   1989
248.4'82—dc20   89-9233
                                                      CIP

Published by Paulist Press
997 Macarthur Boulevard
Mahwah, New Jersey 07430

Printed and bound in the United States of America

Contents

Acknowledgements

I wish to acknowledge my loving family—my Mom, Maura, Joseph and Miceal. They always support me in all I do, and from them has come all the spirituality and loving that I write about.

My thanks to the staff and students at the Institute in Culture and Creation Spirituality in Oakland, California who encouraged me to write and who provided much of the material for *Year of the Heart*—the year I spent with them.

The book was written at St. Mary's in Walnut Creek near San Francisco. The priests there were the best of companions. Fr. John Mallon, renowned for his hospitality, gave me the freedom of the house; Fr. Larry gave me encouragement at a time of doubt; Fr. Peter gave me his thesis which I have valued greatly; Fr. Donal gave me his friendship and a name for the book; Fr. Dermot gave me many laughs and let me use his new set of golf clubs in the interests of sanity.

In the same house Betty and Rose kept me healthy and human, and Maureen, my great support throughout, acted as my agent while I was away, combining with Georgia J. Christo of Paulist Press in finalizing publication details. Mary Claire and Cathy proofread the text and made valuable suggestions. Kathy Shea was always ready to discuss the topics and themes that make up *Year of the Heart*.

The plot for the book was hatched with Theresa, in London, many years ago.

I dedicate this book, dear reader,
to your heart.
And I bless your special friends who
keep it dancing inside you following its rhythms and its dreams;
who keep it young and creative and full of passion;
who keep it empty and full and daily surprised;
who keep it free and proud and delighted with life;
who keep it compassionate in winter and grateful in summer;
who keep it green and bright with Love's image.
Yes. I bless your special friends who keep loving you into
your beauty.

The Master became a legend in his lifetime. It was said that God once sought his advice. "I want to play a game of hide-and-seek with humankind. I've asked my angels what the best place is to hide in. Some say the depth of the ocean. Others the top of the highest mountain. Others still the far side of the moon or a distant star. What do you suggest?"

Said the Master, "Hide in the human heart. That's the last place they will think of!"

—ANTHONY DE MELLO

"Where do we begin?" asks Meister Eckhart.
"Begin with the heart."

Introduction:
Seasons of the Heart

In these reflections I have chosen the heart as the symbol of the mysticism of creation. Around this unifying center a pattern is woven where the many shades and shapes of creation-centered spirituality find a new, positive and simple design. The heart-motif draws on some popular insights from the worlds of psychology, science and theology in the effort to offer this introduction to a secular, incarnational and creation-centered model of spirituality. One of the aims of the presentation is to offer a basis for an intrinsic, holistic and dynamic alternative to a dualistic, limiting and static understanding of Christianity.

Like the welcome arrival of dawn after hours of confused darkness, a way of being holy in a sacred world has once again been rediscovered. Creation-centered spirituality is bringing vitality and hope to individuals, communities, the earth and the cosmos itself at a time when contemporary devotions still follow a privatized model distanced from social and ecological concerns.

This vibrant, challenging and exciting way of being human has powerful support in traditional theological and scriptural sources and in current research and developments in the fields of psychology, science and cosmology.

The content of the following reflections is based on a selection of some significant moments in a person's journey along the passages of life through the seasons of the heart. The heart is a rich symbol for carrying some of these moments in the process of self-actualization where a heightened awareness of the mystery of creation and one's own place within it is reached. The heart is forever dying to itself in its total commitment to its work, but only to give birth continually in another beat of life. The healthy heart's concern is with pumping precious life to places and spaces around and outside itself, thus receiving and giving in the most amazing example of the mystery and paradox of creation.

The purpose of the heart in our bodies is to make sure that each of our cells has enough oxygen. That means the heart must continually pump twenty-four trillion red blood cells to the lungs, where they combine with oxygen. They then return to the heart, where they are pumped to all the outposts of the body. To accomplish this near-miracle the heart, about the size of a large fist, beats 100,000 times day, 365,000,000 times a year. Most of what the heart does is still a profound mystery.

The word "heart" is a tantalizing one in that it has an archetypal appeal which transcends all barriers of language, science, culture and religion, yet can be used in so many different ways ranging from the sublime to the ridiculous. It is a primal word incapable of being properly defined. Yet certain properties of the reality to which it is pointing may be indicated and reflected upon psychologically, scientifically and theologically. It certainly signifies the person as a whole in all bodily and spiritual realities, and resists attempts to dichotomize or departmentalize the human person.

"Heart" taken in this elemental sense denotes that centre which is the origin and kernel of everything else in the human person. It is here that the whole concrete nature of humanity, as it is born, blossoms and spends itself in mind, body and spirit, is crystallised and set; here it is, as it were, anchored. It is the focal place of a

person's primal and integral relations with others and with God. For God addresses his graces to the heart of humanity.
—NICHOLAS HARNAN

This blossoming is imaged here in terms of four seasons or paths that are identifiable in most of the awakenings of the human spirit. The ground plan of the four paths is drawn from the essential thought of Meister Eckhart, the fourteenth century theologian whose vision has influenced mystics and thinkers since that time. The current widespread interest in Eckhart's ideas and writings is largely due to the work of Matthew Fox, also a Dominican priest, whose writings have influenced these reflections.

The creation-centered approach as identified by and retrieved from the medieval mystics is best described as consisting, in general, of four paths. The first, the Via Positiva, applies to the experience of our own divinity and our acknowledgment of this wondrous gift. We respond, with amazement, to the creative energy that blesses the cosmos with unconditional love. The second path, the Via Negativa, describes the silence and emptiness that encourages us to let go of selfishness and to let Love be love within us. It is an entering into the darkness where pain is allowed to be pain and illusions are destroyed. Out of this space of nothingness, the third path, the Via Creativa, is entered into. It brings new energies and empowerment. We participate consciously in co-creation with God. Delight is taken in things green and new, things fresh and growing. The "letting go" has borne fruit and the harvest is heavy. The fourth path is called the Via Transformativa. The conspiracy for change is underway. The pursuit of justice and peace through compassion is entered into. The heart, in community, celebrates, believes and transforms.

This book is set against the backdrop of these four paths or seasons of the heart. Because these four moments of growth are not necessarily linear or sequential, any "Season," or indeed any "month," can be read on its own. Because the turning seasons and months of the year carry a variety of emotional associations for readers in different parts of the world, I sometimes found it difficult to link these "moments" with the moods of the heart in a universally applicable way. For instance, in the rural community of western Europe the harvest time of September and the subsequent leisure time of October are filled, for many, with a perennial sense of awakening and wonder. For others, this awareness may be associated with Springtime which, of course, blesses our land and our hearts with intense newness. I hope you enjoy the journey through the following pages. May it bring you as much joy in the reading as it brought me in the writing.

As we set off, let me add a final word of explanation. Throughout the book I have varied the images of God (father, mother, lover, friend, etc.) as found in the Hebrew and Christian Scriptures. Sometimes, therefore, I have referred to God in the feminine as seems appropriate when reflecting on divine birthing, power and wisdom. Many people's prayer-life is enriched by the recovery of this fine tradition of imagery and language.

HEART'S AUTUMN

A Time for Wondering

❧

Many people sleep through life. For some, however, there is a great awakening. Everything is then experienced differently. "Toto," said Dorothy in *The Wizard of Oz,* "I have a feeling we're not in Kansas anymore." There is a shift in focus. And a second wave of wonder flows across our souls. We listen in awe to the stories about ourselves and we struggle to believe. Are we really here because of an exploding fireball twenty-five billion years ago? Has the Love that gave birth to that terrible beauty actually become human and is that Love in love with me? How much truth can our hearts carry?

SEPTEMBER

The Awakening Heart

> Oh friend, I love you; think this over
>   carefully! If you are in love,
> then why are you asleep?
>
> —KABIR

Is there anything I can do to make myself Enlightened?
  As little as you can do to make the sun rise in the morning.
Then of what use are the spiritual exercises you prescribe?
  To make sure you are not asleep when the sun begins to rise.

—ANTHONY DE MELLO

The Awakening Heart

Most of us are searching for our true selves. Very often we are afraid of what we may find. The search has to do with our anxiety concerning how unloved or unlovable we are. We hope to establish some kind of self-value or self-worth with which to identify. Many psychologists would hold that during our childhood years we may have been exposed to what is called "conditional love." This is an affection that is "earned" through conformity with the expectations of those who tried to shape our lives. During those impressionable years we can mistakenly come to believe that certain experiences, feelings and parts of ourselves are unacceptable and even very bad. And thus the great destruction of childhood qualities begins; slowly but surely the rot sets in. The first conscious fears of losing favor are generated, and the seeds of anxiety about being devalued, losing favor and being rejected by those we love are sown. This is the time, also, when the first psychological "defenses" are set up.

The distrust that is thus engendered stays with us for a long time and sometimes, forever. We distrust ourselves, we distrust others and therefore we distrust God.

By an overuse of defense mechanisms we unconsciously resort to various forms of denial, repression, distortion, and rationalization in an effort to shut off deeper but threatening levels of our humanity. The sad result is often a very poor sense of self, a shallow emotional life, a too great reliance on our intellectual capacities in order to eke out a self-value from a feverish investment in life's activities.[1]

Our fragile, frightened hearts then begin to grow, not out of love and truth, but out of shape and out of reach. In our efforts to escape from and cope with our damaged environment we construct distorting barriers and hurtful devices to protect us.

All of us use defenses; they are essential for our psychological survival. But the greater the range, frequency and intensity of defenses, the more difficult it becomes to get in touch with the reality of ourselves and to alter it in an authentic and appropriate development. If our life is dominated by these defenses, we are far away from our true self and therefore from the capacity to accept and love ourselves and allow others to love us.[2]

Our quest is for the whole and holy heart, the healthy and human one that still beats to its original rhythm. This quest involves the rediscovery of the lost trust already referred to. We begin to dismantle our deep defenses by regenerating a faith in the goodness of God's creation around us and within us. We will then make some headway in revealing the unspoiled face of our heart in all its pristine wonder, made as it is, in the image of Love herself.

To do this we might have to reclaim areas of ourselves that have been rejected and gently bring them into the light of truth. It might also be a profitable exercise to examine the design of the self we are following at this moment. Is it an unloving and uncaring imposition of someone else's design which makes our lives less fruitful and open, which makes us too anxious for the approval of others? Areas of excessive shame and guilt must somehow be submitted to the healing influence of truth even if it means reaching for professional help. Sometimes the source of our shame and guilt is simply in the fact that we are human and have certain human needs and feelings. Above all we must learn that we have all the worth and significance we need *within us*.[3]

This lesson will be learned when we let go of the many deep anxieties we carry within us concerning our value and lovableness. And this "letting go" can only happen when we become convinced of how truly precious we are, the creation of Love, the incarnation of the beauty of God. These "open secrets" lying in the nest of our heart will only come to light when we allow the truth to touch us and pierce through our intricate defenses, releasing our spirit to emerge and dance in the joyful celebration of a new awareness.

God's Seed

Right away I will strike the first note in a theme that will permeate this book—that of the "divine indwelling," first of all in creation itself and then in each of us personally. The penetration of all creation by the love of God is an ageless doctrine and an endless experience. Like children lost in wonder at the excitement of each new discovery, many of us, deeply moved by Love's revelation, are forever amazed at each glimpse of God's extravagant gifts in the passing and the deepest experiences of the days and decades. We are called to recognize, in the ordinary and the strange, in the joy and the pain, in the straight and the twisted, the coming of the kingdom of God. This linking of the timeless with time is, according to T.S. Eliot, "the occupation of the saint." For this awakening of our hearts to happen, this vision of the way things really are, a new stillness must enter our lives. The recognition of the connections comes only with discipline and contemplation—the occupation of the saint. We are called to readjust our shape somehow if we are to reoccupy our appropriate place in the scheme of things. To begin to understand all we must let go of fear. As we will reflect upon later, at length, such a "letting go" is inspired by trust. Wisdom surrenders herself only to those who believe in her. To maintain clear insight we must always be on the journey inward with a trust in the child's spirit within and in the spirit of the wider cosmos all around. Only then, and often in confusion and pain, do our hearts begin to wake up. The simplicity and closeness of Love, as sure and as slow as daybreak, begins to reveal herself to the hesitant but trusting heart. In the "letting go" of so many important certainties we find ourselves left with just one deep hope—that we are loved unconditionally always and everywhere by an enchanting Love of intense beauty and charm. This exciting love affair is kept alive by eternal vigilance. "It must be fought for on the edge of a razor, and it must be fought for every day." These may be fighting words, but I can find no others. Because at the end of the day, literally and metaphorically, it is one long bloody battle. In a finite creation where, in time and space, growth can only happen through engagement with some kind of resistance, the dark forces of diminishment will not readily or easily relinquish their power over the soul to so alluring and liberating a rival. The other side of fear is free love.

I begin this book, this journey we are setting out upon together, with reflections on "the awakening heart." Some hearts do wake up during the long sleep of life. They become aware of mystery—of a love and meaning at the heart of life. This heightened sensitivity is both new and old. Maybe because words are often too clumsy to deal with mystery, it is the artist—the poet, the painter, the sculptor—who preserved the original vision intact. Today this vision of the divine indwelling, of the inter-connectedness of all creation, is being recovered by students of theology and spirituality; it is also being discovered anew by scientists and physicists around the world. It is also, of course, complete, safe and sound, but mostly asleep, in every human heart.

The mystic will put it this way, "The seed of God is in us.

Now the seed of a pear tree grows into a pear tree; and a hazel seed grows into a hazel tree; a seed of God grows into God."[4] A poet uses words this way:

> . . . nature is never spent;
> There lives the dearest freshness deep down things;
> And though the last lights off the black West went
> Oh, morning, at the brown brink eastward, springs—
> Because the Holy Ghost over the bent
> World broods with warm breast and with ah! bright wings.[5]

The book explores this holy presence and sustaining love that empowers the cosmos and everything in it to evolve relentlessly into the future. It reflects also, on how we attempt to explain and envision the human awakening to the reality of this daytime dream. As we ramble in and out of the seasons and pages of the story we will reflect on three dimensions of the mystery as the day begins. There is the letting go and the growing, involved in the emergence of the true, hidden self, precious and valued; there is the letting go of selfishness in the service of the human community in light of a new grasp of our bondedness as a family; and there is the pain and happiness in a commitment to the Body of the cosmos following on our realization that humans are the children of that same Body which is, in turn, the Body of God. Permit me to end this introductory section with some reflections on these three faces of the mystery from a Christian point of view where I will refer explicitly to the Easter event. As I write this during Holy Week 1988, I realize that for many others of different traditions, this too is a time of the turning of the seasons and the symbol of archetypal transition when the world celebrates with light and fire, with water and breath, the perennial circle of conflict and harmony, of fear and trust, of the "already" and the "not yet," and of all kinds of seeming opposites.

The Lion Inside

It was Good Friday in Rome. It seemed ages since I had felt the sun on my face. I was sitting outside a cafe on the Via Conciliazione with one eye on my pizza and wineglass, the other on a book. I was reading the following story from Henri Nouwen's *Clowning in Rome*.

There once was a sculptor working hard with his hammer and chisel on a large block of marble. A little boy who was watching him saw nothing more than large and small pieces of stone falling away left and right. He had no idea what was happening. But when the boy returned to the studio a few weeks later, he saw, to his great surprise, a large, powerful lion sitting in the place where the marble had stood. With great excitement the boy ran to the sculptor and said, "Sir, tell me, how did you know there was a lion in the marble?"

As we moved around the Eternal City and drank in the beauty and pathos of the Pietà and the powerful anger of the seated Moses, we understood to some degree the claim of Michelangelo that he was but discovering and revealing the hidden form already complete within the marble. We then traveled out to Assisi and meditated on the special gift of Francis as he, in his unique fashion, penetrated into the inner loveliness of the marginal and rejected of his time, awakening them to their own worth, value, and beauty. Our opening sentence of the book is, "Most of us are searching for our true selves." We have no choice. It is the quest for meaning and happiness, for love and for God. Once we believe that we are fashioned in Love's image, that she designed the cosmos in general and humanity in particular as her home forever, then the allurement is forever. This imprint of Love-made-woman-and-man is always waiting to be recognized, recovered and repaired in all creation. Perhaps most of all the hidden self is most clear in nature and children. There is a unity and integrity, a kind of spiritual wholeness about what and who they are. As for the rest of us, especially the males of the species, a lot of deeply embedded masses of rubble must be shifted before Love's indelible image is set free. And it is only when we have bred our own "lion" that we can recognize the king and queen of beasts in others. It is the story of Good Friday and Easter Sunday when, in a world of viciousness and cruelty, deep calls to deep in the land of our hearts; when our newly found trusting spirits draw forth the deeply hidden graces in others. And to achieve this we must die.

Last night at the Holy Thursday Banquet of Love we knelt down and washed each other's feet. Today we must live the symbol. In the face of the challenging and accusing expression in the eyes of poor and powerless people in this world's "South," as "Northern" Christians we struggle with our consciences, justifying our selfishness and bargaining with God. "How much is enough?" we ask complainingly. Good Friday is a bad day for that question. Because the pain-filled eyes of Christ are revealing the answer—some form of crucifixion. The experience of Easter and of the weekly Eucharist is a troublesome one for those of us who live our lives within the boundaries of a privatized faith. The invitation to come out into a social, historical and incarnational context for loving God could, if accepted, demand too much.

. . . some Christians find themselves today in real anguish. They know in themselves an undeniable sense of call to imitate Jesus

Christ by a concrete identification with those who suffer most in our society. But this, perhaps, goes along with a feeling of being trapped in an affluent life-style. Such persons may feel very uneasy with their own affluence and the whole pattern of their lives.[6]

There is a real disharmony and alienation between the life that is being led and the deepest yearning of the heart, a disintegration between the daily life-style of the person and his or her sense of the direction of God's call. There is a starkness in the following observation that tests the mettle of all potential "servants":

When we go to meet this wretched neighbor in the way that we should, when we care about him without any supporting feeling of instinctive sympathy, when we forgive even while feeling that we are being made fools of by doing so, when we really pour ourselves out without the reward of a feeling of satisfaction and without any return in gratitude, when our very encounter with our neighbor makes us unutterably lonely and all such love seems to be only an annihilating leap into an absolute void, then that is really God's hour in our lives; that is when he is there. Assuming that we don't turn back, assuming that it doesn't get us down, that we don't find ourselves some sort of compensation elsewhere, that we don't complain, that we don't feel sorry for ourselves, that we keep quiet about it, and really accept and commit ourselves to the absence of ground under our feet and to the foolishness of such love, then it is God's hour; then this seemingly sinister abyss in our existence, as it opens up in this hopeless experience of our neighbor, will be the abyss of God himself, communicating himself to us; it will be the beginning of the coming of his infinity, where all roads disappear, and which feels like nothingness because it is infinity.[7]

The third realization to which our hearts are awakening these days is that of our belonging to a community that is wider than the human—the cosmic communion of all creation.

This is a wonder-filled awareness that brings immense grace, fulfillment, and power. A physicist writes, "The universe is a single multiform event. There is no such thing as a disconnected thing. Each thing emerged from the primeval fireball, and nothing can remove the primordial link that this establishes with every other thing in the universe, no matter how distant."[8] Matthew Fox reminds us that primal people understood this deep connection far better than we do. The earth was their mother; the moon, stars and sun their relations; the animals and trees their brothers and sisters; all people were sons and daughters of the creator.[9] It is an awakening to the fact that almost overnight one has inherited a family of new lovers. "We ought to understand God equally in all things," writes Meister Eckhart, "for God is equally in all things. All beings love one another. All creatures are interdependent."[10]

We have slept long enough. And so much has been happening. It is time to wake up to a new vision of the old world—a world to be loved and saved. "O human being, why do you sleep? Why do you have no taste for the good works which sound in God's ears like a symphony? Why do you not search out the house of your heart?"[11]

NOTES

1. Nicholas Harnan, "A Spirituality of the Heart," *New Review,* Vol. 2 No. 1 (1983) p. 32. (I am indebted to Nicholas for many of the ideas throughout the book.)

2. Jack Dominian and Ann Peacock, *From Cosmos to Love* (London: Darton, Longman and Todd, 1976) pp. 56–57.

3. Harnan, p. 33.

4. Matthew Fox, *Meditations with Meister Eckhart* (Santa Fe: Bear and Co., 1983) p. 28.

5. Gerard Manley Hopkins, "God's Grandeur," *Collected Poems*

of Gerard Manley Hopkins (London: Oxford University Press, 3rd edition, 1949) p. 70.

6. David Edwards, *Human Experience of God* (London: Gill and Macmillan, 1984) p. 100.

7. Karl Rahner, *Mission and Grace,* quoted in *New Review* (1986) Vol. 3, No. 2, p. 3.

8. Brian Swimme, *The Universe Is a Green Dragon* (Santa Fe: Bear and Co., 1985) p. 59.

9. JoAnn McAllister and Matthew Fox, "Creation Spirituality: Education and Essence," in *Breakthrough,* Global Education Associates, (1987) Vol. 8, No. 3–4, p. 54.

10. Fox, p. 26.

11. Adelgundis Fuhrkotter, trans. *Hildegard von Bingen* (Salzburg: Brief-Wechsel, 1965) p. 109. Quoted in Matthew Fox, *Illuminations of Hildegard of Bingen* (Santa Fe: Bear and Co., 1985) p. 28.

OCTOBER

The Wondering Heart

Be patient with all that is unsolved in your heart. Try to love the questions themselves like locked rooms and like books written in a foreign tongue. . . . Live the questions raw.

—RAINER MARIA RILKE

From that day onwards every moment brought me its freshness as an ineffable gift, so that I lived in an almost perpetual state of passionate wonder.

—ANDRÉ GIDE

The Wondering Heart

Sauntering along the Autumn avenues and kicking up the fallen leaves is like walking through a giant's breakfast bowl full of huge cereal flakes—an experience filling our hearts again with wonder. Deep within the dying year the Way of Creation is already being built. And deep too within my dying year I am being re-created. In his book *Let This Mind Be In You,* Sebastian Moore leads one to the conclusion that if we could experience in our heart our own creation we would at the same time experience in absolute fashion how lovable and desirable we are. William Barry[1] too asks whether the heart can experience its own creation in some manner. On the face of it, he writes, the questions seem absurd because automatically we think of creation as belonging to the past. But God's creative act is never over; if it were, we would not be. With such an understanding of creation the question takes on present meaning. If we could experience our creation, then we would have the foundational consciousness that we are seeking. Sebastian Moore points to experiences of a welling-up of desire for "I know not what." The desire is for the unnameable, the "all," the "mystery."

In his autobiography *Surprised by Joy,* C. S. Lewis writes:

As I stood before a flowering currant bush on a summer day there suddenly arose in me without warning, as if from a depth not of years but of centuries, the memory of that earlier morning at the Old House when my brother had brought his toy garden into the nursery. It is difficult to find words strong enough for the sensation which came over me: Milton's "enormous bliss" of Eden comes near it. It was a sensation, of course, of desire; but desire for what? Not, certainly, for a biscuit-tin filled with moss nor even (though that came into it) for my own past. And before I knew what I desired the desire itself was gone, the whole glimpse withdrawn, the world turned commonplace again, or only stirred by a longing for the longing that had just ceased. It had taken only a moment of time, and in a certain sense everything else that had ever happened to me was insignificant in comparison.[2]

There is something about the young heart in its wonderment that possesses a readiness for the experience of some kind of continuing creation that is not always available in later years. Childhood is precious and enduring then, not because within it lie the seeds of maturity to blossom later, but because it is full and, in a sense, already mature in its original vision.

My first remembered experience of the numinous occurred when I was barely three. I recall walking down a little cul-de-sac lane behind our house in Shropshire. The sun was shining, and as I walked along the dusty lane I became acutely aware of the things around me. I noticed a group of dandelions on my left at the base of the stone wall. Most of them were in full bloom, their golden heads irradiated by the sun, and suddenly I was overcome by an extraordinary feeling of wonder and joy. It was as if I was part of the flowers, and stones and dusty earth. I could feel the dandelions pulsating in the sunlight, and a timeless unity with all life.[3]

And Dylan Thomas returns again to the wonder of the heart when, with magic words, he awakens a half-remembered existence;

. . . And I saw in the turning so clearly a child's
Forgotten mornings when he walked with his mother
Through the parables
Of sunlight
And the legends of the green chapels

And the twice told fields of infancy
That his tears burned my cheeks and his heart moved in mine.[4]

Speaking to Sam Keen, Willi Unsoeld, who was on the American team that first climbed Mount Everest, recounted that when he was returning from the peak he paused on a high col to admire the view. Turning around he saw a small flower in the snow. "I don't know how to describe what happened," he said. "Everything opened up and flowed together and made some strange kind of sense. And I was at complete peace. I have no idea how long I stood there. It could have been minutes or hours. Time melted. But when I came down my life was different." "It can happen anywhere, anytime," Keen continues.

The shock of wonder is an earthquake that changes our perception of ourselves and the world and rearranges the foundations of our identity. Explanations, myths, ideologies crumble like so many sand-castles. When the shock recedes, we are left with a memory of having been in the presence of the holy, the awesome and fascinating mystery (mysterium, tremendum et fascinans of Rudolf Otto).[5]

But for many the doors of perception are closed too soon and nighttime comes while it is yet morning. No longer do the encrustations of sophistication fall away but become a wall behind which we hide. Albert Einstein outlines the challenge in staying open, wonder-ful and creative:

A human being is part of the whole, called by us the "universe," a part limited in time and space. He experiences himself, his thoughts and feelings as something separated from the rest—a kind of optical delusion of his consciousness. This delusion is a kind of prison for us, restricting us to our personal desires and to affection for a few persons nearest to us. Our task must be to free ourselves from this prison by widening our circle of compassion to embrace all living creatures and the whole of nature in its beauty.[6]

Why are we so shocked by wonder, when it is what we are made for? Why is the mystic's glimpse always so fleeting when we thirst for more? Why is that extraordinary moment of boundary-melting so rare when it signals our eternal destiny?

Maybe it is the compassionate face of Love unable to wait for our slow return, offering the reassurance that the deeper we penetrate into the mystery of our individuality "the further we travel into the unifying beyond of the cosmos." "Trust me," the Mother is saying, "and trust your own great heart. It beats in tune and time with mine."

Mechtild of Magdeburg, an extraordinary woman mystic of the thirteenth century, wrote so movingly of this divine allurement where God captivates our hearts with a true lover's patience.

> The rippling tide of love
>   flows secretly out from God
> into the soul
> And draws it mightily back
>   to its source.[7]

My image here is of a wracked spirit stretched on the rocks of pain during the night of the soul. And silently, like a baby's breath, the quiet low wavelets flow under and past the empty heart, surrounding it with the rising water of intense compassion. With the breaking of dawn and of the pain the sufferer is caught in the returning undercurrent and borne on the backwash swell to the oceanic center of divine love. And there the moments we have been looking at go on forever.

My intention in this meditation on the wondering heart is

to open the way for a fresh apprehension of the mystery of creation and to unblock some freeways for new images and insights to lighten our hearts. In this section I have three "moments" of creation in mind. The first, concerning the "beginning" of creation, will soon be glanced at in the Cosmic Heart. The notion of continuing creation we have just touched upon, equally briefly. I would like to turn now to a third reflection, on one way of anticipating the "shape" of creation to come.

It was on the verge of the Yorkshire moors in a lovely part of England at a Passionist monastery in Ilkley that I listened to Fr. Barnabas Aherne talking about heaven. Full of the excitement of the post-Vatican Council optimism, we had gathered on a warm summer day in the 1960s and I still remember my delighted surprise when he asked us to consider the possibility of a continuous evolution of this universe into the reality of heaven, rather than a sensational end to all that goes on down here followed by a migration into a new eternal homeland. He gave examples from time, space and individual growth. He spoke of this future astonishing mystery of almost unimaginable proportions in terms of transcendence. It was truly wonder-ful. While in a sense most of us believe that heaven and hell somehow begin here "below," now we were listening to a careful, theological argument for such challenging propositions based on the scriptures and tradition. My wonder was full of reverence. What an incredibly extravagant explosion of love and power. Twenty years later it is still so exciting to listen to scholars from other disciplines shedding more and more light on these amazing possibilities. In his exploration through science and philosophy into *The Seven Mysteries of Life,* Guy Murchie very carefully considers a possible paradigm for the future of the evolving planet as the story of creation continues to unfold. After critically examining the "law of transcendence" insofar as this can be accomplished on many fronts, he sums up these multiple aspects:

. . . individual transcendence in which each of us develops larger and larger awarenesses of space, time and self, social transcendence in which individual consciousnesses are absorbed into superconsciousness or a group mind and world transcendence in which the consciousnesses and superconsciousnesses of nations and empires on a planet evolve into a world superorganism that ultimately conveys them beyond the finitude of space, time and self toward the Infinitude of Mystery in the Universe, which may be called God. All of these transcendencies are more or less interinvolved as far as I can tell, but if you'll pardon a suggestion, one could clarify the whole process in one's mind by thinking of the familiar mortal space-time field on Earth as something that extends or expands radially outward along with one's personal consciousness toward an invisible, intangible and abstract continuum in which one's fellow beings are somehow never born and never die, but just ARE. . . .

(Thus) finitudes transcend into Infinitudes, mortals into Immortals, matter into mind into Spirit and, just possibly, creatures into their Creator.[8]

The Heart of Christ

Theologically speaking, everything that I have written or will write in this book, either by way of fact or speculation, about the three "moments of creation" (referred to above)—the initial happening in time and space, continuing creation and the shape of things to come—is drawn from my understanding of the revelation of God in Jesus Christ, which, in the cosmic calendar, is not so very long ago. I see the mystery of the Incarnation as the "showing forth" of the love and meaning in the heart of Love when it gave birth to this amazing world and everything in it. That is why I think it appropriate to briefly explore this awesome truth (from one particular point of view) in this section of The Wondering Heart.

It is enriching and rewarding beyond measure to reflect on the mystery of the Incarnation as a cosmic event as well as a historical one in time and place.[9] Most Christians tend to think of the Incarnation as a unique event, an intervention of God in the history of humanity, distinct from the wider mystery. Redemption is often regarded as a kind of rescue operation on God's part—an intervention at a moment in time to salvage a world gone adrift. Theology, cosmology and spirituality are searching for a common dancing rhythm at this crucial point. Theologically, a rather narrow, extrinsic, reparation-centered view of redemption has given way to a more traditional, rich and intrinsic, incarnational meaning. From the point of spirituality, a privatized model of devotion—a Jesus-centered kind of piety—has surrendered to a more universal and creation-centered understanding of the fleshing of the Word. And cosmologically, instead of reducing the Christ-event to a mere second-thought "plan B" type of temporary interruption of the evolutionary unfolding "to save the chosen people," we are now challenged to enter more deeply into the mystery of Incarnation and explore it as the culmination and fulfillment not only of a promise to a few, not only of all human history, but of the whole universe, the mysterious cosmos as well. Our interest lies, just now, with this third consideration regarding the cosmic Christ. Let me explain what I mean.

The elements which make up the human body, and therefore the body of Jesus in his mother's womb, were being prepared when the original explosion of the matter of the universe took place. We now know that the appearance of the galaxies, of the stars and of the sun, and finally of this planet Earth, were all stages in the evolution of matter which was to lead to the appearance of life on earth. Life on this earth again developed over millions of years to produce plants and animals, until finally the point was reached when consciousness emerged within humanity. At this point the universe became conscious of itself. In short, "our ancestry stretches back through the life-forms and into the stars, back to the beginnings of the primeval fireball. This universe is a single multiform, energetic, unfolding of matter, mind, intelligence, and life. And all of this is new."[10]

Each one of us, then, inherits a body which has been molded by billions of years of evolution from protoplasm to animal and finally awakes to consciousness as a human being. It was the same with Jesus in the womb of his mother. He was linked like every human being with the whole history of cosmic evolution. In him too, a human emerged which was capable of thought, of feeling, of language and gesture, of a distinctively human life.

Just as we have a physical inheritance from the first matter of the universe, so also we have a psychic inheritance from the first person. All humans are linked not only physically but psychologically with one another. In our emergence into consciousness we enter too into a cosmic consciousness, inheriting the awareness of self which has been developing in humanity from the first beginnings of human existence. Each of the traditions to which we belong, racial, linguistic, cultural, is a branch of the wider human evolution. Every child inherits certain archetypal images and patterns of thought which have been developed throughout the centuries of history. All of this exciting story applies to Jesus Christ.

Jesus in the womb of his mother inherited the "psyche" of a Jewish boy. His mind was molded by the forces which had created the family of David and the people of Israel, and beyond that, his consciousness reached back to Adam, from whom like every human child he was descended. We have to recognize therefore that Jesus was a child of his time. He had the body and mind of a child of the first century. His understanding of God and creation were determined by his heredity. There is nothing in the gospels which indicates that he had any human knowledge which was beyond the compass of the Hellenistic Judaism of his time.[11]

And there is more. Beyond the body and the soul, there is in every human being a spirit, a pneuma which is the current and link, not only with nature and humanity but with the Great Spirit of Love itself. The spirit is the all-pervasive presence in humanity of the Spirit of God. This pneuma is a readiness, a capacity for self-transcendence. There is in every human being a power of self-transcendence, a potency for going beyond the limits of mind and matter, to experience what Rudolf Otto called the "holy mystery." This potential for growth into divinity is always intrinsic to human nature whether recognized as such or not. It has been called by many another name from the beginning of our history. Briefly, the story goes like this. Because God is love he wished to express that love, to give it birth in time and space. This whispered word of love we call the cosmos, and within the cosmos there is humanity, and within humanity there is this part of God, this aptitude, this allurement, this demand almost for transformation and total union with Love herself. The intensity of the attraction varies from person to person. In some it burns low. In Jesus it was a consuming flame, the brightest light that ever rose to meet the parent fire that rages in its Mother. Put in rather stiff theological language it reads like this:

In Jesus of Nazareth the self-communicating presence of the mystery we call "God" and our own personal quest reach the highest level of intensity; they meet never to be separate; they meet as one. Jesus is subjective human personhood and subjective divinity as one. On the one hand, the self-disclosure of God driven by love pushes outward until she becomes the object of her love—the human being. At the same time, the self-transcendence and openness characteristic of each man and woman find a special intensity in Jesus of Nazareth. [12]

And this is a cosmic event. In this human being we all become aware of our incredible identity and destiny—as daughters and sons of God growing into total union with Love itself. Just as the emergence of consciousness in humanity was a cosmic event, so the awakening of the Spirit within, raising this consciousness to another level, spiritual awareness, is a further stage in cosmic evolution. This stage has already been reached in Jesus. He is the One in whom the cosmic evolution attains its end. "It has pleased God," St. Paul writes, "to bring all things to a head in him, things in heaven and things on earth."

A transforming power has been released throughout the universe penetrating the whole of creation. All has been lifted to a new level of love. As scientists today recognize, the universe is an interdependent whole, a time-space continuum. Nothing happens in any part which does not affect the whole. In the Incarnation therefore, the reality and the destiny of the universe has been revealed. The Christian can now reflect upon creation in the light of the Incarnation and see that what happened chronologically later was primary in God's intention. In Christ is celebrated the ecstatic announcement and epiphany of the loving purpose and meaning of the cosmos. "Let me express myself in even a clearer way," writes Meister Eckhart. "The fruitful person gives birth out of the very same foundation from which the Creator begets the eternal Word or Creative Energy and it is from this core that one fruitfully becomes pregnant." He writes too of God's loving mercy: "Jesus became a human being because God the compassionate One could not suffer and lacked a back to be beaten. God needed a back like our backs on which to receive blows and thereby to perform compassion as well as to preach it." How lovely are those words!

During Heart's Autumn we urgently coax into life our sleepy hearts. "Make ready for Christ," shouts Thomas Merton, "whose smile, like lightning, sets free the song of everlasting glory that now sleeps in your paper flesh, like dynamite." And in the silence of that cosmic night, when we behold above the holy animals, the dancing angels playing with stars, 'tis not the whispered beating of a tiny drum we hear; it is the rhythmic gurgle of a happy God in time and tune within a baby-heart . . . at last . . . at last . . . at last . . .

A baby heartbeat with cosmic echoes. Because the small mystic would grow bigger soon and reveal an undreamt-of intimacy with the all-powerful force of life. I suppose no other word in history has collapsed as many universal and cosmic separations and alienations as the reverent and unique word "abba."

NOTES

1. William Barry, "Experiencing Creation," *The Tablet,* Nov. issue (1986) p. 1276.

2. C. S. Lewis, *Surprised by Joy,* quoted in Barry, op. cit. p. 1276.

3. Edward Robinson, *The Original Vision* (Oxford: Religious Experience Research Unit, 1977) p. 49.

4. Dylan Thomas, "Poem in October," quoted in O'Leary and Sallnow, *Love and Meaning in Religious Education* (Oxford: University Press, 1982) p. 107.

5. Sam Keen, *The Passionate Life* (San Francisco: Harper and Row, 1983) p. 193.

6. Albert Einstein, quoted in Michael Nagler, *America without Violence* (Covelo, CA: Island Press, 1982) p. 11.

7. Sue Woodruff, *Meditations with Mechtild of Magdeburg* (Santa Fe: Bear and Co., 1982) p. 93.

8. Guy Murchie, *The Seven Mysteries of Life* (Boston: Houghton Mifflin, 1978) pp. 517, 518, 497.

9. Bede Griffiths, "The Incarnation as a Cosmic Event," *The Tablet,* Dec. 26 (1981) p. 1242. (I am indebted here to the vision of this fine mystic.)

10. Brian Swimme, *The Universe Is a Green Dragon* (Santa Fe: Bear and Co., 1984) p. 28.

11. Harnan, p. 34.

12. Thomas F. O'Meara, "Theology of Revelation," *Theological Studies* Sept. (1985) p. 422.

NOVEMBER

The Cosmic Heart

As the heart is to the body
so are we to the cosmos
. . . and to God.
—Daniel Dancing Fish

In the beginning was relationship.
—Martin Buber

The Cosmic Heart

This section is full of surprises and requires an open heart since it entails a certain amount of "letting go" where deep-seated opinions are concerned. I will begin by telling a story and then we will "do" some theology.

The story is about how the world was made. It is a cosmic story about the origins and development of the universe. It is about the emergence of the galaxies, the stars, the planets, light, and all living creatures. It is a revolutionary story that can only be half told. We do not know the ending. But from what we do know of it, we can learn about the strangest happenings of extraordinary creativity, variation, abundance and beauty. It is a new story. I tell it at the beginning of the book because this story will shape our lives especially in terms of our spiritual sensibilities and personal sense of responsibility. Above all it provides the spiritual energies for the whole human community to begin to live according to the dictates of the story. It has urgent implications for the human race. It forces us to think in a new way, to be conscious and to BE at a richer level because we realize that evolution is now internalized and our inner consciousness is the key to the future development of the universe.

Once upon a time—rather at the beginning of time—there was a great silent fire. And this fire was the spirit of Love containing within it the seeds of everything that was to be born ever. From this fire we can trace the unfolding, through a dramatic variety of sequences, the form of energy, of matter in the first generation of stars, the birth of life on planet earth and finally, human consciousness itself. And all this still goes on . . .

Every point of the cosmos was a point of this exploding light. Incredibly, we can still see this first light as it reaches us now after a twenty billion year journey. It is this primal energetic moment of fire and light—mysteriously erupting from the womb of emptiness and nothingness—that I refer to as the cosmic heart. And it is this eternal cosmic heart that thunders and whispers the lifebeat for all, the mightiest and the frailest.

The scientists can now assure us that everything that exists in the universe came from a common origin. Our ancestry stretches back to the beginnings of the "primeval atom." This unfolding of matter, life and intelligence still goes on. The universe, in fact, has poured into us the creative powers necessary for its further development. My creativity is essential to the unfolding of the universe. To learn about creativity we must begin to understand the creativity of the earth; to discover the meaning of ordinary things we must establish ourselves within the evolving cosmos as a whole. This demands study and careful reflection before we realize that we (humans) are "the latest, the most recent, the youngest extravagance of this stupendously creative Earth."[1] So often we see ourselves as almost totally distinct from the universe, but in fact we are the self-awareness that provides the space for the universe to feel its own breathtaking beauty. In the words of Julian Huxley, quoted by Teilhard de Chardin, "humanity discovers that it is nothing else than evolution become conscious of itself."[2] The earth, like God, needs and demands a thinking heart to reflect back its unique loveliness and to wonder at the miracle of it all. The universe has waited so long and now calls out to us and rejoices beyond measure at its self-awareness in reflexive humanity. Brian Swimme, the renowned physicist, compares the Earth without a human to a child without a parent.

I sometimes think the primary deed of a parent is to see the beauty and grace of children. Children are magnificent, gorgeous beyond telling. They themselves have no idea of what beauty they embody. Can you see the tragedy of a child with no one to feel and cherish its beauty? No one to fall in love with this magnificent creature? No one to celebrate its splendor?[3]

From the planets' point of view, according to Swimme, we can say that the Earth is awakening to its own beauty, power and future possibilities.

Before continuing with my story, let me highlight just three aspects of this emerging mystery that have become lodged in my heart. The initial explosion sent matter erupting outward in all directions. The explosion itself is remarkable. Scientists like Sir Bernard Lovell tell us that

if the universe had emerged a fraction of a second faster or slower it would have exploded in such a way that it could never coalesce into galaxies at a later stage or it would have collapsed back on itself. So in its initial moment, a sacred moment in the epics of most peoples, the universe came into existence at a slim—almost zero—margin of possibility. This fact, and the many other extremely important transformations, like that from non-life to life, which again took place at almost zero possibility, tell us something about the fragility of the universe.[4]

The fact that we know so little about this incredibly beautiful story and that we take so many mysteries and miracles for granted indicates that we have much work to do in sensitizing ourselves to the Mother from whom we have strayed so far.

Another thought-provoking revelation concerns the fact that the sequences of transformation which form the story of the universe are irreversible. We are so used to life forms renewing themselves through birth and the sequence of the seasons that we seldom reflect on the irreversibility of the evolutionary process. Yet, as Teilhard puts it in the *Phenomenon of Man*: "Once and once only in the course of its planetary existence, has the earth been able to envelop itself with life. Similarly, once and once only has life succeeded in crossing the threshold of reflection. For thought as for life, there has just been one season."[5] This revelation adds another new and fascinating dimension to the background of the story and of our very existence.

The third point I wished to make concerned the profound impact that this awareness can make on our soul-life. There is a sense in which one cannot be the same again having heard the story. One's self-awareness, one's spiritual life, one's way of being present to God, to the world, to others—all are deeply transformed in the receptive listener. This book is about such a transformation. But it's getting late. Let me finish the story.

Cosmic Attraction

The ultimate goal of cosmic evolution is the becoming of love in human form. Brian Swimme writes about love as allurement and attraction. The basic dynamism of the universe is the attraction each galaxy has for every other galaxy. The ultimate mystery of the falling rock and the revolving Earth—the mystery of the gravity that is an attracting activity—remains unsolved no matter how intelligently we theorize. This primal alluring activity is the basic reality of the macrocosmic universe.

When we hear the word *love* we think only of *human* love, a very special sort of love. So I am certainly not saying that gravity is human love. I *am* saying that if we are going to think about love in its cosmic dimension, we must start with the universe as a whole.

We must begin with the attraction that permeates the entire macrostructure. I'm speaking precisely of the basic binding energy found everywhere in reality.[6]

Teilhard stresses this affinity of being for being as a property of all life. If there were no pressure for simple molecules to unite "it would be impossible for love to appear higher up with us, in hominized form." Human love is the highest expression of this communion. It embraces the world of nature, the network of human minds and ultimately Love herself.

The transformative power of love is now pushing human consciousness to reach up and achieve a new level of union at Omega point. The communion and love that binds all reality together reminds us that all living forms are in reality members of one large family, so that in a very real way we are brothers, sisters and cousins.[7]

Moving into the complex interplay of human relationship we can also begin to understand that the mysterious attraction we call "interest" or "fascination" is as amazing, as basic, as the allurement we call gravity. "The great surprise," writes Brian Swimme, "is the discovery that something or someone *is* interesting. Love begins there. Love begins when we discover interest. To be interested is to fall in love. To become fascinated is to step into a wild love affair on any level of life."[8] Destiny unfolds in the pursuit of individual fascinations and interests. The unity of the world rests on the pursuit of passion.

In his book *To Care for the Earth,* Sean McDonagh tells the New Story, as he puts it, of Teilhard's vision and hopes that it will become the scaffolding for a powerfully unifying force among the total Earth community in the early twenty-first century. But in order to capture people's imagination, the story will need to be told, he says, not just in the abstract form of scientific language, but "it will have to be sung, set to music and painted in such a way that its beauty and grandeur can lure us away from the life-destroying story that now grips us."9

Father McDonagh is right. The implications of the story for each one of us and for the world itself are immense. We begin to see ourselves in a startlingly new and dynamic way.

You do not know what you can do or who you are in your fullest significance or what powers are hiding within you. All exists in the emptiness of your potentiality, a realm that cannot be seen or tasted or touched. How will you bring these powers forth? How will you awaken your creativity? By responding to the allurements that beckon to you, by following your passions and interests. Alluring activity draws you into being, just as it drew the star into being. Our life and powers come forth through our response to allurement. . . . You will carry within you the complexity of the world in a manner unimaginable to your previous self. You will know that you are not disconnected from the life of the world, nor from struggling humanity in all its difficulties throughout the planet.

You will learn the first glimmer of the profound manner in which humans bind together the entire social order through a heightened awareness of what it means to be a compassionate human.10

Brian Swimme is trying to impress upon us the power we have to evoke being, to enhance the life around us as we ripen into love's activity, as we pursue our destiny with the same extravagant devotion of the star to its destiny. The desire to make us over into love is permeating the universe. We are initiated into love when lured into the intense pursuit of "the enchanted lover."

In recent years, however, human beings have not been at ease in the natural world. Both story-tellers to whom we have listened have continued to grieve over and warn us about the unbelievable destruction that we are inflicting on our Mother, the defenseless Earth. It is a sad and shameful part of an otherwise enchanting and bewitching epic. I will return to this vitally important theme in The Dark Heart.

Tremendous Lover

The question I struggle with at this point is the "why" of creation: Why was creation desirable or even necessary? Much of our inherited theology does little to help us here. There is a strong dualistic strain in the opinion that God somehow "condescended" to create the world and did so as a wound-up kind of clock that was left to tick out its life (with the occasional interference from God) until the end of time. (One of the tragic side-effects of such a creation-story is the divine indifference to the Earth that it falsely portrays, giving the impression that the world exists solely to be used as a resource by human beings. Thus, a weak and even misleading Christology that does not establish and protect the divinity of all creation provides no defense against the relentlessly powerful and destructive forces of evil within humanity that are plundering this lovely world, even as I write these very words.)

Let us look at the above question through different windows. Theologically, one can assume that Being or Love, mysterious and infinite, pre-existed the fireball and the "primeval atom." I like to think that God could contain herself no longer and created out of passion. Since all creation is in God's image we can explore the ways of life, and work back to the divine source. (This kind of play is called "doing theology," especially when it springs from group reflection.) All created love yearns toward "making flesh" in some form or other. The world is full of small incarnations as creatures forever search for appropriate expressions in time and space of the emotions that rage through their hearts. Lovers, for instance, create words, gestures, symbols and babies as concrete, "sensible" manifestations of their love. Thus it was with God. "Bonum est sui diffusivum." It is because divine love, in the first place, has to be fleshed through creating and begetting that we, Love-coded as we are in God's fertile image, continue to express her nature. We are Love, in time and space in human form, evolved through the aeons in a history of startling beauty and rich mystery.

How could such an exquisitely captivating story of love have lost its charm, color and allurement over the centuries? Or what strange winter froze the erotic juice in the male hearts, turning a tale of enchantment into a dry theology? Oh what a loss those dark powers caused, and how many have lived and died and never knew how special, precious and beautiful they were in the passionate eyes of the tremendous Lover herself. Just as surely as today's children will be severely deprived of basic joys tomorrow because of our desecration of nature, we are now suffering the withering consequences of a male-dominated theology in the past. Cut off from the life-giving greening power of rich feminine imagery and vision, the divine-human love-story weakened and died. What greater proof of this than the refreshing, rushing words of a great woman, Hildegard of Bingen.

Out of the original source of true Love in whose knowledge the cosmic wheel rests, there shines forth an exceedingly precise order over all things. And this order which preserves and nourishes everything comes to light in a way that is ever new. . . . It is Love which here properly distinguishes and moderately adapts the powers of the elements and of the other lofty assortment associated with the strength and beauty of the world as well as with the entire physical structure of humanity. . . . Out of this true love which is totally divine, there arises all goodness, which is to be desired above everything else. Love draws to itself all who desire God, and with this impulse Love goes to meet them.[11]

"You shine so finely," she says, "you are encircled by the arms of the mystery of God."

Moving to another window for a different view of the same first moment, we join Sam Keen, a writer, teacher and feminist of note. Somewhat fancifully, he imagines the mystical body of Being-becoming-Itself, incarnate in the cosmos, as itself the climax of an act of love. The theory, he thinks, is wild enough to be interesting and salacious enough to surprise theologians and scientists. In support of his "theory" he writes:

Under the microscope, the atom looks more like a love-nest than a machine shop. The manly nucleus sits at the center of a kingdom, emitting a positive, musky charge. Electrons, like dancing girls, whirl and tease in orbit and keep their distance by a negative charge. Clearly, desire binds them together in a love dance. Scientists, not wishing to suggest that anything pornographic is going on among basic particles, have discreetly agreed to call the communion of particles by a single name—atom. In fact, there is no atom without an Eve, no plus without a minus, no yin without a yang. The least particle we know is already an organized bit of energy engaged in active intercourse with other particles.[12]

Like a folded tent inside us to be, one day, opened out, set up and lived in, God's seed is implanted in our hearts and from this outpouring we will grow and flow unerringly onward into the divine Being.

Guy Murchie is gazing through another window. In *The Seven Mysteries of Life,* a massive work of exploration in science and philosophy, the author briefly addresses this question. Having carefully examined the fascinating data about initial creation and the consequent evolution of life, Murchie philosophizes about the reason for such a phenomenon in the first place. Could it belong to the *very nature* of wisdom and love, he asks, to have a beginning sometime, someplace, and from there to sprout and grow? He is referring here to divine love and wisdom as well as human mind and spirit. Some kind of viable world setting is called for if God's love is to come into existence as developing mind and flowering spirit.

Thus emerges a basic reason for time and space, which together make possible form and motion, without which meaning could hardly be understood. For form is an alphabet of sorts which makes possible language, including mathematics, and particularly the numbers needed to measure and define geometric form. This, I have a hunch, just may be the why of the whole material world, which appears to be a principal finite aspect of the greater mental-spiritual world—an aspect enclosed in mortal space-time fields especially designed for the evolution of spirit, which may show first through the faint feelings of plants, next the stronger senses of animals, then, with expanding consciousness, transcending toward thinking, while feeling and thinking gradually coordinate and blossom into a spiritually mature whole—which, from there, can further evolve and exuberate onward toward attributes and powers and joys and heavens we cannot yet imagine![13]

Further on he returns to the theme and describes our earthly life as a tentative tuning in . . . a transcendent resonance, a harmonic, a geometric interval, a note in a song of eternal and incomprehensible mystery.

For limitation is essential to measurement, to contrast, comprehension, articulation. Just as an artist must limit his choice of paints if his picture is to have meaning, or a message must begin and end if it is to be understood, so life must have impact, adventure, form and feeling if it is to fulfill its purpose. Without letters printed sharply enough to be sensed, the page of life is blank.

So the spirit-mind associates itself with finity in order to grow. It makes its entrance upon the stage of a material world. It assumes form in order to learn meaning. It assigns itself to a position in space and time so it can measure things and grasp the shape of ideas, visualize relativity, and feel the warmth of love. How else, in basic terms, could it learn anything or develop itself? Where else is wisdom to be sown but in some sort of a world—and what is a world without some kind of form to define its existence?[14]

Transfixed at yet another window is the physicist Brian Swimme. His stunning little book captures the essence of his extraordinary vision where the scientific and the spiritual intertwine to weave design after design of breathless beauty. Throughout these reflections, a subtle duet builds the artistic bridge between the language and concepts of physics and theology to shed some more light on our question. He regards the wind as an epiphany of the earth. With reference to the second law of thermodynamics he sees this epiphany as revealing the cosmic dynamic of expansion out from an area of high concentration. So too with love and allurement, although the basic, scattering fragments of gravity, attraction, instinct, magnetism, will be called by different names in the various sciences and disciplines. God, the tremendous Lover, experiences an irrepressible need to give expression to his deep delight and joy. Creation was an outburst of celebration, an explosion of love, a symphony of extravagance and a gracious and beautiful work of art. As we touched upon already, all this celebration, surprise, extravagance and artistry becomes self-aware in us. We are called to become the heart, the mind—the space—where the God become Cosmos celebrates and plays her existence. There is an innate urgency in Love to give birth to time, place and space at the beginning and, having become the Universe, to continue birthing and creating in ever more unexpected and imaginative ways in the only way he can do so now—in and through us. And at this point we realize that maybe our question should never have been put. To ask such a question weakens one's powers. Only the neophyte asks it. The query comes from the sidelines, not from the center where the actors are totally engrossed in the white heat of play.

You never have to ask anyone else what or why to celebrate; the dynamic of celebration celebrates, that's all. Self-expression is the primary sacrament of the universe. Whatever you deeply feel demands to be given form and released. Profound joy insists upon song and dance. Don't ask anyone what to celebrate; don't even ask yourself! Let celebration be. Let generosity of being happen. Nothing more is required.[15]

What is needed is a new way of being human in this new Earth. We are dis-eased because we are rootless. We have lost our sense of belonging. We are living unnaturally, out of touch with the power that the universe is aching to set free in us. Nature isn't even second nature to us. But the signs are good and we still have time. There is a collective gathering of intent; an intuitive conspiracy of readiness; a time of waiting before a profound happening. It is the moment before some kind of revelation. It has something to do with trust. In the meantime we will not forget. Around us there is the land, the sky at night, the rivers, the plains, the four directions, fire and lightning . . .

You can come to establish yourself in a relationship with the mountains so that to glance at them is to be reminded of the cosmic dynamic of memory. The mountains and the rocks shout ceaselessly: REMEMBER! Whenever water rushes over your body, it brings into your presence the reality of cosmic sensitivity and our destiny as the mind and heart of the universe. When the wind blows coolly in your face, you are feeling the activity of generosity, reminded of the great joy and destiny of celebration. And whenever you feel sunlight on your arms, you are reminded of that great cosmic flame, the unseen shaping of which permeates you and connects you to the embryogenesis of the Earth.[16]

In my first draft of this section I had finished here. On rereading the material I was taken by surprise. I realized in a deeper way how right Brian was about not asking the question "why" in terms of celebration. It is enough to BE to celebrate. "Why" does not come into it. We celebrate simply because we ARE. And then, of course, I also understood Meister Eckhart's admonition more clearly, too. "This I know," he said, "that the only way to live is like the rose—which lives without a why . . . because life rises from its own foundation and rises out of itself. Therefore life lives without a reason. . . ."[17] I reflected again on these words and astonishingly I realized that we had, almost by accident, come round fortuitously to the original question about God's reason for creating! And of course! It is a non-question. Neither did God have a reason, a "why." God *is* creation. To be God *is* to be birthing, outpouring and flowing, shining and extravagant, loving and playing. God *is* life-giving greenness, empowerment and surprise. God IS . . .

NOTES

1. Brian Swimme, *The Universe Is a Green Dragon* (Santa Fe: Bear and Co., 1984) p. 31. (I have relied heavily on Brian's lectures and book for the material in this chapter.)

2. Julian Huxley, "Introduction to Teilhard de Chardin," *The Phenomenon of Man* (London: Fontana Books, 1959) p. 243.

3. Swimme, p. 32.

4. Sean McDonagh, *To Care for the Earth* (Santa Fe: Bear and Co., 1986) p. 83.

5. Teilhard de Chardin, *The Phenomenon of Man* (London: Fontana Books, 1959) p. 30.

6. Swimme, p. 45.

7. McDonagh, p. 96.

8. Swimme, p. 47.

9. McDonagh, p. 96.

10. Swimme, pp. 51, 52.

11. Matthew Fox, *Illuminations of Hildegard of Bingen*; text by Hildegard of Bingen with commentary by Matthew Fox (Santa Fe: Bear and Co., 1985) p. 41.

12. Sam Keen, *The Passionate Life* (San Francisco: Harper and Row, 1983) pp. 246, 247.

13. Guy Murchie, *The Seven Mysteries of Life* (Boston: Houghton Mifflin Co., 1978) p. 496.

14. Murchie, p. 519.

15. Swimme, p. 147.

16. Ibid. p. 150.

17. Matthew Fox, *Meditations with Meister Eckhart* (Santa Fe: Bear and Co., 1983) p. 30.

HEART'S WINTER

A Time for Waiting

&

To learn how to wait, how to be silent, how to befriend
the dark . . . Thus do we prepare to be creative. There is a
waiting, a silence and a darkness in all birthing. Heart's
winter is already a filling womb. In these reflections on the
Via Negativa I have also acknowledged that our spirit suffers in the reality of life—a reality that is no stranger to the
demonic power that inhabits our heart. For the font of
inspiration and newness to keep welling up within us,
these wounds and this evil must be encountered and
owned. So that creative love may flow in and out, each
heart, one day, must be broken.

DECEMBER

The Silent Heart

The Master insisted that what he taught
was nothing; what he did was nothing.

His disciples gradually discovered that
Wisdom comes to those who learn nothing,
unlearn everything.

That transformation is the
consequence not of something
done but of something dropped.

—ANTHONY DE MELLO

. . . we grow by subtraction . . .
—MEISTER ECKHART

The Silent Heart

"Ah sure, 'tis the silent words that tell a greater story." In this reflection I wish to write about the power of God's silent words in our silent heart.

Words, we often think, serve to break the silence. However, maybe it is silence that serves to complete the words. The quality of the words determines the quality of the silence, and in silence, as all lovers know, we edge closer to what we love. Precious and beautiful as our best words are, their most effective contribution is toward the revelation that happens in silence.

But only the well-prepared and brave heart can risk traveling through the strange spaces of silence where many wild things, beautiful and dangerous, live. Because in stillness all kinds of shapes and shadows creep out of hiding and awful wordless wars are waged—between the deep guilt in our lives and trust in reconciliation; between accusation and defense; between nearness and distance; between holding on and letting go; between staying in and reaching out; between fear and love. In our timeless time of silence when the busyness, routines and distractions of the veneer of each day are stilled and seen for what they are, then frightening forces threaten us. I refer here to a hollowness, disgust, boredom, weakness and wretchedness that rise up to envelop us—but not to destroy us. The point to remember is that for many of us this is a necessary and redemptive time. There is a saving grace paradoxically at work in the uneasy emptiness and dead distance always and already at the doors of our hearts that silence reveals. Without this nameless remoteness we would, so to speak, come home too soon in this world, commit ourselves too quickly within the finite, leaving no space for the wild spirit of transformation and creativity that must never be domesticated.

"The Word lies hidden in the soul in such a way that one does not know it or hear it. Unless room is made in the ground of hearing, it cannot be heard; indeed, all voices and sounds must go out, and there must be absolute silence there and stillness."[1] The fourteenth century Dominican, Meister Eckhart, was well aware that the silence is to hear the voice of Love, the stillness is for listening to the whispers of mystery. There is no passivity here, no mere absence of sound. The dynamic in the silence is one of "letting go": it is the creating of space in the interests of receptivity, the emptying before the filling, the pause before the music, the moment before the breath. It is a "making room" for a deeper awareness of God. "Silence means the letting go of all images—whether oral ones or auditory ones or visual ones or inner ones or cognitive ones or imaginative ones. Whether of time or of space, of inner or of outer. It is a radical letting go of language."[2]

As he probes the mysterious meaning of Incarnation, the Jesuit scholar Karl Rahner reminds us that this feast is about the nearness and distance of God experienced in silence. It is a quiet festival of the heart where the openness of each one and the love of God draw near; a celebration in the fine point of the spirit where self-giving Love from without and receptive experience from within meet and dance in mutual and enriching understanding and vision. The restless hollowness which surfaces into our consciousness when we reflect in silence is already the nearness of God. "He is there," writes Rahner,

like the pure light which, spread over everything, hides itself by making everything else visible in the silent lowliness of its being. The Incarnation urges us, in the experience of solitude, to trust the nearness—it is not emptiness; to let go and then we will find; to give up and then we will be rich.[3]

When the quite startling implications of Incarnation occur to us in silence, our fearful hearts are threatened. The human and the divine must be kept apart. The unredeemed dualism spawned by our pristine fears reasserts itself with relentless stubbornness. We struggle for the shallows when we sense the pull of a powerful current that might drag us into a great unknown and uncharted ocean. Still in the grip of some elemental and sinister dynamic we prefer to keep Love at a distance. It is safer that way. We are afraid to *let go* of ourselves in God and to *let God be God in us.* But the Incarnation actually happened. After a long wait we can now explore the boundless sea of God's love—the last barrier between the human and divine has given way. God has allowed the divine self to be reached and possessed by humanity's questing spirit for the absolute—the free spirit implanted by God in the first place in the heart of humankind. God wishes to be lost in us. Men and women are the absolute openness for God's own self which cannot be given in any more total way than by creating us in a fashion that allows us to be capable of freely receiving this divine self in its generosity and extravagance. "God is the prodigal who, in fact, squanders himself/herself," writes Rahner, "and when God lets himself go outside himself then humanity appears." So God has become man and woman, child and non-human life. The world and its destiny are now a part of God's very self. Now we are no longer watched by Love as a spectator; the life of this Love is our life too. "Now I shall tell you something I have never spoken of before," confides Eckhart. "God enjoys herself. In the same enjoyment in which God enjoys herself, she enjoys all creatures. God finds joy and rapture in us. . . . If I spent enough time with the tiniest creature—even a caterpillar—I would never have to prepare a sermon. So full of God is every creature."[4]

We no longer, therefore, seek God in the endlessness of a bewildering beyond where our tired spirit loses its way. God is no better off than we are, struggling with and in us, in no way specially privileged, hungry, weary, frightened and killed. That the infinity of God should take upon itself human narrowness; that joy should accept the mortal sorrow of a fallen earth; that life should take on death—this is the most unlikely truth. And this is why we light candles at Christmas.

We light them because we sense that now God has spoken into the heart of the world, the silent word of the last, the deepest, the most beautiful and loving reality of divinity in Incarnation. Through the birth of this child everything is already transformed. All hope is already real possession. God is already possessed by the world. All wisdom is within our grasp now because its source is firmly rooted within the human, graced spirit. All bitterness is only the reminder that it is not yet clearly known that the one universal revelation has happened; and all the happiness of this earth is only the mysterious confirmation, still lost on most of us, that Love is already and always at home in the heart of all creation. "For God is at home," explains Eckhart. "It is we who have gone for a walk." The celebration of the Christian Incarnation is the grateful "yes" of the world to its union with God. Its experience is that of divine love humanizing us at our deepest center.

The Great Mystery will draw closer and begin to reveal some of her secrets in silence. We hope, in the emptying that silence is, to discover a way of being present to what happens and to what is. To be totally open to apprehend the full impact of each moment and each encounter the heart must be set free from all prejudices, pre-conceptions and expectations. The silence at the center of our reflections here is for emptying and for letting go of the images and knowledge that obscure the vision of our hearts and our ability to truly hear.

Wherever this Word is to be heard, it must occur in stillness and in silence. . . . There we can hear it and understand it correctly, in that state of unknowing. Where we know nothing, it becomes apparent and reveals itself . . . people should be as free of their own knowledge as when they were not yet, letting God accomplish what God wills. People should stand empty.[5]

The point being made here is that the winning of this inner freedom is hampered by the baggage of an inherited knowledge that often clouds our awareness of things. What is to be aimed at, and what is "the occupation of the saint," is the ability to experience and observe each moment without a pre-established mind-set that prevents us from being sensitive to the integrity of all that we perceive whether "ugly" or lovely. This mental stripping of oneself of all that pre-conditions us to judge and assess what happens to us is difficult and hazardous. What is to be fostered is a sense of consideration, watchfulness, patience and compassion. To appreciate fully what *is* one must discipline oneself into a condition of simplicity whereby the mind is unfettered by a kind of ephemeral knowledge which is often inculcated unwittingly in the home and school by religious and secular authority. To apprehend the full flavor of life as it flows into us, to appreciate with gentleness the creative joy of living, we must question and challenge the kind of security that is often provided by secular code and religious creed and traditional expectations. Certainty and unexamined convictions are ambiguous in the extreme. In our clinging to them we miss the many-splendored newness of things. All of these, too, we must let go if we are to become the Love we already sense within us. "There, where clinging to things ends," Meister Eckhart preached many centuries ago,

is where God begins to be. If a cask is to contain wine, you must first pour out the water. The cask must be bare and empty. Therefore, if you wish to receive divine joy and God, first pour out your clinging to things. Everything that is to receive must and ought to be, empty.[6]

Many of our theories, for instance, about morality and religion, which we consciously bring into play to measure the immeasurable reality of what happens, are often a form of security to which we become accustomed and on which we rely; in our silence we are confronted with the conformity and fear that we are generally unaware of each busy day.

Seeing all this, a really thoughtful person begins to free himself from every kind of security, inward or outward. This is extremely difficult because it means that you are alone—alone in the sense that you are not dependent. The moment you depend, there is fear; and where there is fear there is no love. . . . When you are controlled by ideas, isolated by beliefs, then fear is inevitable; and when you are afraid, you are completely blind.[7]

There is a powerful Christian precedent for this kind of dying and discontent, this self-emptying and letting go in the interests of letting life be. This kenosis is the necessary prerequisite for acquiring an amazing new love of all human and non-human life; a love that is open to all kinds of new beauty because it is non-possessive; a love that identifies at source with the streams of living power that enliven all creation. The challenge is to try to understand ourselves and our encounters with life from moment to moment without the process of accumulation, argument and conclusion. Only then can we see ourselves truly to be a part of God, one with her beauty and grace unconditionally and extravagantly blessing us all at every moment. The heart is not free while it is judging, comparing and converting. If there is an aim it is to see everything as new and fresh. To be creative we must, in a sense, become less rather than more. "God is not found in the soul by adding anything," the mystic Eckhart reminds us, "but by a process of subtraction." Another great mystic who died last year put it this way:

Only the mind which has no walls, no foot-hold, no barrier, no resting place, which is moving completely with life, timelessly pushing on, exploring, exploding—only such a mind can be happy and eternally new, because it is creative in itself. . . . But you can only be that when you leave the pool you have dug for yourself and go out into the river of life. Then life has an astonishing way of taking care of you because there is no taking care on your part . . . and that is the beauty of life.[8]

Only Connect . . .

Another dimension of the human heart is that of loneliness. By loneliness I do not mean the condition of sadness or loss that results from a deep relationship which no longer exists, such as one finds in a family or between close friends or lovers. I refer instead to a state of alienation in which most of us find ourselves, being disconnected to a greater or lesser degree, to our own bodies, our environment, our friends and therefore God. The psychic damage we suffer from such separation is all too clear because there is a loving unity which holds all creation together and when that is fractured only deep trouble can follow. Many would hold that it was because of the escalation of this alienation in past centuries, evidenced, for example, by the loss of this vision of cosmology by the Christian churches in the late middle ages, that the world of neurosis emerged so significantly. This, in turn, spawned a flood of schools of psychological theory and practice to repair this spiritual breakdown. When the unifying and loving power of mysticism was neglected and no longer nurtured, a terrible emptiness opened up in the human heart.

How do we restore the mystic to that heart which is lonely and sick without its healing presence?

The mystics of all traditions were keenly aware of the interconnectedness of all creation. ". . . we open ourselves like the air," the native American Gayle High Pine writes,

and the world flows through us like the wind. . . . We have no boundaries—we *are* all we know, experience, feel—all of which interacts with everything, making us of the entire earth. As our bodies do not grow and unfold from choice and decision, neither do our hearts. Through the old ways, we are in harmony with all circumstances—the correct and harmonious course of action is always to be found in us if we are in touch with ourselves.[9]

Our spiritual, mental and physical health depends on the way we structure our world and choose our life-style. Our survival now demands the recovery of an informed and loving relationship with our bodies and our environment. If our carelessness and neglect of nature is not swiftly rectified, the destruction could be terminal. "Either we learn that we are a part of a natural ecology which must be reverenced and loved or we will not survive."[10]

One never fails to be surprised at the rich conviction in the Amerindian traditions regarding the sacredness of the environment. The mystical experiences of great visionaries such as Chief Seattle and Black Elk were shared by most of their people. Nature is personified. She is a beautiful mother with whom her sons and daughters have a loving and dutiful relationship. They are part of her body. She lives in them. Her life and nourishment are freely given to them, and freely, too, their bodies are received back into hers when they die. And she suffers and rejoices on both occasions because there is no eternal death on the plains. The rhythm is true, the dance is round, the circle is full, holy and strong. Each is part of the other—a oneness within the self and with the earth, the animals and the elements. The four directions, the seasons, plant life, the clouds, sun, moon and stars—all are brothers and sisters and relations in a web of sharing. Maria, a young native woman, explains about the way her father begins his day's work.

He holds his hoe, removes his hat and asks permission of the God of the sun—grandfather sun as we sometimes say—so that God will help him. My father speaks to the earth telling it that he will not harm it. It hurts my father to uproot the grass from the mountain which is like clothes for the mountain. He then asks permission to work the land. [11]

Because we are dealing here with mystery, no one culture, tradition or religion has a monopoly over the vision. All speak with an evergreen freshness of joy.

The Upanishads remind us that God's one mystery is his creation of Reality within the cosmos. This is available to anyone, anytime, anywhere because she has enshrined the macrocosm and the microcosm within each other. Therefore, if you know yourself you know the whole mystery. In another place, Swami Jyoti points out:

All things you could understand very well: what the trees are communicating with each other, or the fish or the birds are telling each other. There is not only an ecological but a cosmic interconnection of all things including ourselves. Barriers and divisions are a myth. That all things are in you and you in all things—this is real truth. When you will awaken to that subjectivity you will know the truth and see the beauty and joy in it. [12]

The Christian mystics too have beautiful words and thoughts about this mystery. Hildegard of Bingen writes ". . . everything that is in the heavens, on the earth, and under the earth is penetrated with connectedness, is penetrated with relatedness"[13]; "now God has built the human form into the world structure, indeed even into the cosmos, just as an artist would use a particular pattern in her work."[14] "God has arranged all things in the world in consideration of everything else."[15]

From the perspective of a scientist another light is shed on the mystery.

Sometimes I wonder about the human body's being a miniature replica of the earth's surface. For it resembles our outer planet remarkably, being composed of the same elements in the same proportion: three quarters water, one quarter solids, both organic and inorganic, with swift internal flows, occasional eruptions and gentle daily tides. And there is a corresponding similarity between the atom and the solar system, where the sun represents the proton and the planets the electrons that orbit round it.[16]

Murchie refers us to Bertrand Russell's comparison of a person's existence to the development of a river growing stronger within its banks then rushing passionately past boulders and over waterfalls until finally, having grown wider and quiet, the waters, without any visible break, become merged in the sea and painlessly lose their individual being. He also reminds us of Alan Watt's way of telling the story.

. . . we do not come *into* the world, we come *out* of it, as leaves from a tree. . . . When the line between yourself and what happens to you is dissolved, you find yourself not *in* the world but *as* the world. There is a feeling of hills lifting you as you climb them, of air breathing yourself in and out of your lungs. All space becomes *your* mind. . . .[17]

One final comment here about another image of the way we are all inter-connected by our loving thoughts, and about the potential for growth and change in such a network.

The intermingling of minds within the human species has been compared to a vast plain containing millions of wells that appear on the surface to be independent sources of water but deep underground actually interconnect and combine into tributaries that ultimately become a single mighty river.[18]

Control and Letting Go

There is a great beauty about a wild heart. We are deeply stirred in the presence of a certain kind of "madness." Because within us all there is a longing for release from conformity and routine into strange worlds where permission is always granted to be free and open—where there is another way to live and to be. Unfortunately, in this dispensation, things are otherwise. While the wildness of which I write is subject to its own natural control, I wish to comment now on this characteristic of control in its repressive and negative influences on the lives of us all. I refer, in particular, to the phenomenon of emotional repression and mental rigidity.

There are many reasons for this kind of quarantining of our heart-responses. First of all, culture tends to reward us—especially men—for hiding our feelings, for being stoical, controlled and rational. Second, our religious training excelled in the training of the intellect and will, "the noblest faculties of the soul." Third, all our education, especially in our early home life, reflects many of the above cultural and religious values. "The emphasis was on control rather than on integration of our feelings into our total life experience. Too little time may have been spent on helping us to learn how to feel, how to cope with the sometimes baffling experience of anger, sexuality, the pain of loss and separation." Many of us, in later life, spend so much time in trying to figure out how all this can come about. Most of us will have picked up a sense of disapproval associated with certain feelings (especially of anger and sexuality), and this deeply buried sense of disapproval could give rise to feelings of unexplained guilt, fears of rejection or feelings of being worthless. We did not succeed in meeting the expectations of others. Even in spite of our inner childhood convictions that we were not being true to ourselves in our efforts to please, we played along with the adults' rules for an adults' game. We sensed hypocrisy if not injustice. Once these elemental premonitions and our *feeling* presence in the world became inhibited and under threat, then we were set fair for acquiring control and defense mechanisms such as suppression, pretense and rationalizing and intellectualizing our experience. In a manner of speaking we were forced to become uncomfortable with our wild wee hearts, inhabited by angels and demons of imagination and fantasy, and to live, rather superficially, "in our heads."

Trying to live in our heads is an old way of dying. The heart is starved; the imagination too is undernourished. Because our presence to both our internal and external worlds is not purely intellectual in spite of the world's admiration for the single-minded rational person. We are only half living when the left brain solely is engaged. Such a presence to reality, far from being commendable, is very tenuous, misleading and usually unhealthy. Our deeper self mourns this impoverishment and tries to express this grief in various ways. Much of the suffering contained in certain kinds of depression, anxieties, loneliness and periods of darkness is, in reality, a heartfelt plea calling us back to our deeper, truer selves—our hearts—where Love and Being are imprisoned and long to run free within us, restoring moistness, greenness and healthy growth to our complex and fragile body-spirit.

It is not always easy to eradicate dualism from the dark recesses of our hearts. Part of our nature is drawn strongly toward dichotomy and categorization. The essential unity of creatures and creation is not always obvious to clouded human hearts. So many of us are fragmented and out of touch with our true selves. We divide ourselves into a body and a soul, a mind and a heart, thoughts and feelings, matter and spirit. I have suggested how our childhood experiences may have been responsible for much of this destruction. The task now is to repair the damage. For some it happens so quickly; for others it may take ages of time. But the connections must be re-established; the reconciliation must happen; the domination of the "head" must be transcended; its control must be broken.

In some instances, as I have mentioned already, it is difficult to do this. The channels are fixed and the rut becomes deeper than the grave. Relentless control becomes second nature and even the tiniest hands of skill cannot reach in to dismantle the complex defense mechanism or decode the elaborate combination system. On the one hand there are, as we have seen, the psychological strategies that defy penetration—the sublimation, isolation, denial and projection that take up residence within the house of our hearts. On the other, these subconscious blocks have a corresponding physical peculiarity expressed in the body as muscular rigidity or, in Wilhelm Reich's terminology, as "character armoring." This condition is typified by an immobility detectable in the eyes, the mouth, the neck, the chest, the abdomen and the pelvis. The journey toward integration and wholeness is a long one. But it must be taken. Because deep in all of us there are rich depths of power and wisdom and a sweet stillness, hidden under layers of fears, anxieties and illusions. There are, in spite of the sometimes almost insurmountable difficulties involved, a number of ways of reaching into those depths. Throughout this book we will look at some of these, especially the way of meditation and the way of letting go.

For those of us who tend to live in our heads, a certain kind of "letting go" is as necessary as it is difficult. It is a movement from "head-knowledge" to "heart-knowledge" or wisdom. It has to do with the "humanizing of knowledge," transcending it into wisdom by lacing it with love.

Letting go is never easy. The desire to have, to hold, to possess and to control is part of our nature. But the more powerful part yearns to learn the lesson of growth and openness; to enter the mystery of the secret of loving without desiring; to live in emptiness and stillness and therefore in a state of receptivity and readiness so that the quality of our being and "our being present to" are all that matter.

NOTES

1. Matthew Fox, *Breakthrough* (Santa Fe: Bear and Co., 1980) p. 260.

2. James M. Clark, *Meister Eckhart: An Introduction to the Study of His Works with an Anthology of His Sermons* (London: Thomas Nelson and Sons, Ltd., 1957) p. 162. Quoted in Fox, ibid.

3. Karl Rahner, *Theological Investigations* IV (London: Darton, Longman and Todd, 1964) Quoted in *New Review* (1985) Vol. 4, No. 1, p. 2.

4. Matthew Fox, *Meditations with Meister Eckhart* (Santa Fe: Bear and Co., 1983) p. 14.

5. Karl Rahner, *The Eternal Year* (London: Burns and Oates, 1964) p. 100.

6. Fox (1983), p. 54.

7. Mary Lutyens, ed. *The Krishnamurti Reader* (London: Penguin, 1978) p. 99

8. Ibid. pp. 144, 145.

9. Gayle High Pine. Quoted in Dolores la Chapelle, *Earth Wisdom* (1972) p. 11.

10. Sam Keen, *The Passionate Life* (San Francisco: Harper and Row, 1983) p. 125

11. Maria (no second name given), "We Call the Earth 'Mother',"
Creation (1987) Vol. 2, No. 6, p. 17.

12. Jyoti Amar Swami, *Retreat into Eternity: An Upanishad* (Boulder, CO: Gold Hill Pub., 1981) p. 17.

13. Gabrielle Uhlein, *Meditations with Hildegard of Bingen* (Santa Fe: Bear and Co., 1983) p. 41.

14. Ibid. p. 46.

15. Ibid. p. 65.

16. Guy Murchie, *The Seven Mysteries of Life* (Boston: Houghton Mifflin, 1978) p. 514.

17. Ibid. p. 533.

18. Ibid. p. 517.

JANUARY

The Dark Heart

We would rather be ruined than changed
We would rather die in our dread than
 Climb the cross of the moment
 And see our illusions die.
                              —W. H. AUDEN

Within every heart abide angels and devils . . .
                              —LEONARDO BOFF

The Dark Heart

The reader will have noticed the occasional theological flavor to the reflections I am sharing. I wish to begin this section with some thoughts about the reality of sin. I trace most of the following ideas to an evening in early January while I walked by the side of Killarney's Middle Lake. I remember a mistiness, stillness and strange emptiness as night came early across the sleeping lake. What clarified itself for me was a new understanding of the meaning of sinfulness. This was more profound and urgent than the definitions and descriptions I grew up with. It is often felt that proponents of incarnational theology and creation-centered spirituality have a flawed awareness of sin. Beginning with Jesus himself, through Irenaeus and Scotus Erigenus, to Teilhard de Chardin and many twentieth century theologians, this accusation has been made. In light of their insight I now see all that works against unity and that tends toward closedness as sinful.

Unmasking Sin

There are many paradigmatic figures whose response, in life and death, to God as lover (cf. The Erotic Heart) was so open, unifying and thorough that something of the immense love of God for the world was disclosed. To the Christian, Jesus was one such figure. He is unique to us as our foundational sacrament. "He is our (Christian) historical choice as the premier paradigm of God's love." By virtue of a "continuity" (Karl Rahner) and a "solidarity" (Hans Küng) between Jesus Christ and the rest of creation, all creatures have potential as the beloved of God to respond to, reflect and express the love of the Lover. Leaving aside for the moment the question of whether or not non-human life is the fullest expression of its Maker's will for it, the fact that most human beings are not so is central to my definition of sin: the option for non-growth, the refusal to be the special part of Love's body that we are called to be, a reluctance to strive for the reunity and healing of a fragmented world. There is a mysterious darkness in the heart that defies all scrutiny. It is mysterious in that it exists and is defined by virtue of the light with which it is forever in tension. In terms of sinfulness this darkness is the tendency to hide away alone, to turn away, not from a transcendent power but from community-mindedness and inter-relatedness.

It is not pride or unbelief but the refusal of relationship—the refusal to be the beloved of our lover God and the refusal to be the lover of all God loves. It is the retention of hierarchies, dualisms and outcasts so as to retain the superiority of the self. It is a horizontal refusal to be part of the body of God rather than a vertical refusal to be inferior to God.[1]

The need here for a revisioning of theology and a revolution in religious education is becoming urgently obvious. The sins that concern us are not the sort that can be atoned for and forgotten; jarring moments in an otherwise pleasant melody; inappropriate stammers in an otherwise flawless presentation. They are rather the dark backdrop to a persistent refusal to acknowledge, and resistance to, the call to openness, the radical challenge to let go and trust, the invitation to community and interdependence.

The evil we must deal with, epitomized in our systemic structures of oppression due to race, class, and gender, as well as the deterioration of the ecosphere and the monstrous escalation of nuclear weap-

onry, will not disappear through God's having "conquered" it in
battle. . . . (Consequently) salvation is not something received so
much as it is something performed; it is not something that happens
to us so much as something we participate in. This implies a very
close relationship between soteriology and ethics; that we are made
whole only as we participate in the process of making whole. We
participate then in our own salvation.[2]

For more than a decade of preaching, unaware of the dualistic premise of my argument, I interpreted this last statement
as heretical. In recent years I have understood that:

salvation is not a 'second work' of God; it belongs intrinsically to
the 'first work'—creation. Salvation is a deepening of creation; it
says to all, even to the last and the least, not only, "It is good that
you exist" but also, "You are valuable beyond all knowing, all
imagining." The saviors of the world are lovers of the world.[3]

I find it difficult to account for the persistent splinteredness
in "official" pronouncements regarding the meaning of sinfulness and salvation. The very language perhaps reveals the
reason. Reference is usually made to "sins" and "redemption." The reconciliation is between the individual soul and
God. But a revolution in our thinking has moved us away
from non-holistic, non-global thinking. Sinfulness, at root, is
anti-growth, anti-evolutionary. It resists the new, the risky,
the challenge to trust. It lives off a preoccupation with parts.
It thrives on dividing and compartmentalizing. It can only
live within boundaries. Sinfulness is agoraphobic. It cannot
survive in open spaces. Because its gestation depends on individualistic bulimia it has no identity at the communal table of
love. The concentration on personal redemption has allowed
the monstrous escalation of sinfulness to proceed unchecked,
disguised in system, establishment, social and institutional

garb. While recent official Church documents are unmasking the faces of sin in the breaking of the bonding between humans (as well as between the individual and God) there is as yet, in current pronouncements, no indication of the evil inherent in the awful alienation between humanity and the universe. Referring to the 1983 Synod of Roman Catholic bishops on Reconciliation and Penance, Sean McDonagh notes:

The anthropology underlying much of the official Church's approach to reconciliation overlooks any real relationship between what is happening to the Earth and the injustice in human relations. . . . The bishops did not see that the destruction being brought about by acid rain, industrial, agricultural, human, nuclear and chemical pollution will sterilize the planet in as vicious and deadly a way as interhuman conflict and fear.[4]

True reverence is not reserved for special recipients and special occasions: it is a condition of the heart like life is to Being. The stance that people take toward the Earth is of a piece with their stance toward each other.

If their approach to the Earth is marked by lack of respect, arrogance, greed and rapaciousness, then they will also exploit their brothers and sisters. . . .[5]

Identifying Resistance

McFague refers to the place of will in the human attempt to transform the world.[6] When the heart is dark this will to grow, to create, to be new, to transform is missing. We have just been reflecting on this resistance to the call to self-transcendence in terms of human sinfulness, theologically speaking. A psychologist will identify a deep-seated condition of laziness and entropy at the root of such apprehension in the face of the demands of discipline and the challenge of responsibility. "We are accustomed to imagining the experience of conversion or sudden call as an 'Oh joy' phenomenon," writes Scott Peck in lighter vein. "In my experience, however, more often than not it is, at least partially, an 'Oh shit' phenomenon."⁷ When our hearts are dark they lose perspective and balance. There is an unhealthy obsession with self. Far from being true self-love, the dark heart denies its own beauty and cannot celebrate its power and responsibility. Matthew Fox points to the resistance "to fall in love with life, to love what is lovable, to savor life's simple and non-elitist pleasures, to befriend pleasure, to celebrate the blessings of life, to return thanks for such blessings by still more blessing."⁸ The laziness of the dark heart is the child of fear. The desire to possess is at odds with the desire to be. Because one grows by addition, the other by subtraction. The one is controlled by fear, the other controls fear by trust. One reaches to have, the other to give. One grasps, the other lets go. One knows, the other wonders.

The dark heart is a stranger to vitality, to creativity, to the uses of imagination. One can reflect on the darkness of depression as an absence of divine life and love. The "laziness" referred to has a sinister face—a face without spontaneity or imagination; a face incapable of being surprised; a face that never smiles; a face that offers no clue toward the identity of its divine parentage. When the heart is dark, the artist is dead, and no healing happens. The awfulness of this condition of inertia and acedia is in the absence of power, compassion and the will toward justice. Evil thrives, not when the weaker people do evil things, but when others do nothing. There is no participation in the loving transformation of the community of creation, by such a lost heart. In "The Green Heart" I offer some reflections on the shadow side of personality. This is a vast topic of immense importance, and I can only make suggestions for further reading in the bibliography at the end.[9]

Acknowledging Evil

One hot summer in the 1970s I was "standing in" for my brother as chaplain to a large hospital in Manchester, England. Visiting a psychiatric ward certainly concentrates the mind. One night I was called to talk to a patient who had, according to her doctor, certain "spiritual" problems. She thought she should be perfect. That was how she interpreted the Roman Catholic exhortation to be always in "the state of grace." A particular brand of piety which has spawned the notorious torment of "scruples"—the relentless desire for endless confessions, the debilitating sense of guilt, the inordinate fear of hell and a whole series of prohibitions and taboos—had driven this poor woman, and very many others, into an acute state of anxiety. It is a long journey backward first, and then forward, into the land of love where all such fear is cast out, together with the neurotic condition and the psychosomatic ailments which a rigid, coercive and infantilizing legalism can produce.[10] It is a "catch 22" for many of these wounded believers because, after a certain stage had been reached, it is only the system that has trapped them that can set them free.

This woman really did not stand a chance. Her understanding of love was based completely on her experience of home, church and school. These three most powerful influences spoke only of conditional love. At home she lived to please her parents, her true self going into hibernation for a long, long winter. The destructive repression continued at school, as she obediently "performed" for her teachers. Whenever the spontaneous and trusting child risked coming out to play it was wounded again and again. At church she carefully learned how to merit God's love. If you were "good" you won his favor and graces. But if you were wild or "different" you incurred his anger. Most natural inclinations as expressed in thoughts, desires, and actions were dangerous temptations or at least venial sins. By this time the damage is well-nigh irreparable. The enchanting experience of unconditional love as pure gift is probably out of reach forever.

There is a type of devotion which leaves us defenseless in the face of living with our sinfulness and coping with the conflict between good and evil which forever rages within us. This dangerous lack of awareness of the reality of the human condition has led to a locating of evil somewhere outside ourselves, in various categories of "bad" people, for instance, and in a personification of evil as an external devil whose address is not our own. This is where the trouble starts.

And the damage along the way is incalculable, because people are rendered defenseless in the face of evil. Their power is given away from the beginning when their divinity was never preached. The wretched weakness of the human condition was indelibly imprinted in receptive young hearts as, for some, Sunday after Sunday, every shred of dignity and pride was carefully dismantled from the holy shrine of childhood. All confidence in the inner self was systematically eroded and drained away because no one knew that the human heart was filled to the brim with the wild explosive power of God's dynamic love. Most of this book is concerned with exploring the "divine indwelling" with reference to the human, the universal and the cosmic. I wish to reflect here on the various shades of darkness within us too, with special reference to the reality of evil.

It is difficult to identify and accept the disguised evil alive and well, deep within ourselves. We can spot it easily in the world at large. "But," observed Gandhi, "the real devils are those running around in our own hearts . . . and only there must the battles be fought." In his fine little book about St. Francis, Leonardo Boff writes,

Within every great saint there lives a great demon. The roots of sanctity are born in the depths of human frailty. Virtues are great because temptations conquered were great. One is not nursed on sanctity like mother's milk during infancy. Behind the saint is hidden a person who has conquered the hells of human nature and the crush of sins, despair and the denial of God. They have fought with God like Jacob, and they have been marked by the battle. . . . Sainthood is the reward for a painful battle won. Within every heart abide angels and devils. . . .[11]

There is no gainsaying the strange power of darkness and evil that permeates and influences all our deepest aspirations, conscious and unconscious. St. Paul himself was no stranger to this condition when he wrote about the profound resistance to doing good that he felt within himself. The traditional doctrine of original sin serves to remind us of this fundamental fact of our human experience. While often negative, pessimistic about human nature, and unbalanced in its emphasis, nevertheless the catechism focus on the weakness of the will, the darkness of the understanding, and the strong potential for evil in all people testifies to this basic contradiction in all of us and offers an important warning to those who would deny the ambiguity of their humanity in search of an angelic nature.

In his classic *Markings,* Dag Hammarskjöld reminds us that:

. . . we can reach a point where it becomes possible for us to recognize and understand Original Sin, that dark counter-center of evil in our nature, that something within us that rejoices when disaster befalls the very cause we are trying to serve or misfortune overtakes even those we love. Life in God is not an escape from this; it is the way to gain full insight concerning it.[12]

The challenge then is to face the dark corners of our own hearts. This is never easy. If, in the past, a sense of personal sinfulness was overstressed, today many prefer not to recognize the capacities for chaos within us, let alone confront them.

Man must become relentlessly aware of the potentiality for good and evil within him, taking care not to think that the one is real and the other illusory. Both are true as possibilities in him. He cannot completely escape from either if, as he should from the outset, he lives his life without self-deception.[13]

If we run away from evil without understanding it through experience, we risk becoming blind to its full reality, above all its destructive power in ourselves. The fear and avoidance of evil leads to neurosis. Sheldon Kopp in *If You Meet the Buddha on the Road, Kill Him!* writes, "By recognizing this evil in myself, and by satisfying it in fantasy, I decrease the possibilities that I will find some devious ways of living it out with other people. . . . As a result, I am usually free of the temptation to try to manipulate and control others surreptitiously." To identify the evil and the goodness within us and to arrive at the interface between the darkness and light is a significant moment in the quest for wholeness and integrity. In a most mysterious way, we both identify and dis-identify with these two dimensions of ourselves. What is mysterious is the strange need we have for the demon in our lives. It is in our struggle with the devil, our wrestling with the demon of resistance, that the womb of tension is set up from which flow the children of our creativity. It is, we know, in such moments that God is eternally bringing forth new life. Without the tension and resistance of the stretched and strained string there would be no pure music. "As the Godhead strikes the note," Mechtild said, "humanity sings. The Holy Spirit is the harpist, and all the strings must sound which are strung in love."[14]

The issue therefore is complex and requires much reflection. In *The Way of All Flesh* Samuel Butler wrote: "People divide off vice and virtue as though they were two things, neither of which had anything of the other. This is not so. There is no useful virtue which has not some alloy of vice, and hardly any vice which carries not with it a little dash of virtue. . . ." I remember listening to a most impressive human being, a bishop of the Orthodox Church, Metropolitan Anthony, as he spoke to us during Lent in the elegant Waldegrave Drawing Room of St. Mary's College, my Alma Mater, in beautiful Strawberry Hill, on the banks of the proud old Father Thames. "After Mass one morning," he said, "a woman approached me bursting with good news. 'I have acquired almost all the virtues,' she panted with holy glee, 'and am now left with only two vices.' 'For God's sake,' I replied, 'hang on to those two vices. . . .' "

The acceptance of the experience of evil, then, can lead to knowledge of the good. There may be more than a grain of truth in the suggestion that in facing up to our "shadow side" we are at the same time setting free those deeper dimensions of our being in which are rooted many of life's most enriching qualities, such as artistic sensibilities, inspiration, compassion and the intuitive faculties of the spirit.

I write this as we approach Holy Week, a time of deep significance for Christians. Indeed, for many cultures and religions, and for no human-made reason, these weeks represent a time of symbol and play when light and darkness weave and sway in cosmic combat, and good and evil—those elemental and universal powers of destiny—scatter the planets in their eternal dance of war. The ultimate victory, we are told, may well be assured, but our personal struggle with the night-time of our souls continues in each of us, and the social battle too, against the many faces of evil, must be waged until the final transformation is achieved. Only the God who is love itself knows the hidden skirmishes that are fought every day in our "ordinary" lives under the veneer of getting on with each day's measure of pain and joy. We ache to strike back when we are hurt, to get even when we are let down, to destroy and even to kill in the face of infidelity, betrayal, or tragedy. The liberating news for the Christian lies in the cosmic drama played out in the special child of the universe himself, Jesus Christ, when the dark evil that stalks the pages of the story of creation was harnessed and controlled. The elemental celebration at the hour of Easter Vigil embraces the whole universe and reverberates throughout all creation. Because the healing, reconciling, and completing grace and power that bring integration, growth and compassion to all life are symbolized, affirmed and intensified in that frail and twisted body, with its sweat of blood and its hidden smile of peace.

NOTES

1. Sally McFague, *Models of God* (Philadelphia: Fortress Press, 1987) pp. 139–140.

2. Ibid. p. 145.

3. Ibid. p. 146.

4. Sean McDonagh, *To Care for the Earth* (Santa Fe: Bear and Co., 1987) op. cit. 177.

5. Ibid. p. 178. (The whole of this book emphasizes the intercon-

nectedness that harmonizes and transforms. See also *Manifesto for a Global Civilization* under Fox in Bibliography, and also McFague, ch. 5.)

6. McFague, p. 213 (note 22).

7. Scott Peck, *The Road Less Travelled* (London: Century, 1987 reprint) p. 305.

8. Matthew Fox, *Original Blessing* (Sante Fe: Bear and Co., 1983) pp. 119–120.

9. The following selections offer a popular introduction to the topic in question: William Miller, *Make Friends with Your Shadow* (Minneapolis: Augsburg, 1981); Janice Brewi and Anne Brennan, *Celebrate Mid-Life: Jungian Archetypes and Mid-Life Spirituality* (New York: Crossroad, 1988); Adolf Guggenbuhl-Craig, *Power in the Helping Professions* (Dallas: Spring Publications, 1971).

10. Pierre Solignac, *The Christian Neurosis* (London: SCM Press, 1982)

11. Leonardo Boff, *St. Francis: A Model for Human Liberation* (London: SCM Press, 1985) p. 131.

12. Dag Hammarskjöld, *Markings* (London: Faber and Faber, 1964) p. 128.

13. Jolandi Jacobi, *Masks of the Soul* (London: Darton, Longman and Todd, 1976) p. 121.

14. Sue Woodruff, *Meditations with Mechtild of Magdeburg* (Santa Fe: Bear and Co., 1982) p. 87.

FEBRUARY

The Wounded Heart

> How strange a mystery
> that God's most precious gift
> when incarnated
> emerges as
> suffering.
> —Daniel Dancing Fish

. . . He is breaking me down into his own oblivion to send me forth on
a new morning, a new man . . .

—D. H. Lawrence

The Wounded Heart

"Aho Mitakye Oyasin," prayed Buck Ghost Horse and another heart-red rock cracked open. Its broken body released intensely questioning waves of penetrating heat in search of truth. There are no liars in a Sweat Lodge. In the darkness, by the ring of fire, our unhealed wounds began again to bleed. Because there was no escape, no distraction. The senses were stilled. Only the truth flowed out, in a river of tears. There was a profound sense of "letting go." My heart seemed at home in the dark. Maybe darkness and fire are the natural setting for the unfolding of mystery—especially the mystery of suffering. Like a heart-sized poultice the pus of my wounds was absorbed into the richness of the emptiness around it. In that tiny tortoise-shaped space, perched on top of a hill in Oakland, I began to trust the sinking silence of the universe. How important that trusting was, how full it seemed! In the letting go of my soul I was letting it free to BE. The unmistakable thrill of falling in love was again stirring in me. This time with the darkness. The ground of my soul was dark and I was taking this darkness and, as Starhawk urged us to do, was dreaming it into a new image.

I was aware also of a different encounter with pain. I was calling it by name and allowing it to happen. It was coming free and it was not all bad. It was burning, purifying and clarifying as it swept and fire-washed shining the kitchen of my soul. There was something strangely sweet about the pain as I was rolled over and over by this river of power that had burst its banks. It was a state of complete commitment with no place to hide and nothing to hide because nobody was watching. I felt forgiven by creation. And the wounds of my spirit continued to bleed. And it was all happening together.

And the purple points of pain continued to explode against the darkness of my soul like dancing fireworks in a starless night. And barriers collapsed and control was lost from the inside out. Huge cosmic walls kept falling away slowly, outward and downward, and I felt I was becoming nothing in a void of nothingness . . .

As I sit here tonight with Tchaikovsky's Serenade for Strings beating its way through me I can recall the sensations that filled my emptiness in that endless kind of moment. I can identify an intense awareness of beauty, a keen feeling of loss, a sense of pathos that is indescribable and, I think, a new sensation of almost detached compassion. The words of a poem that I had learned by heart as a small boy came back to me because my heart had remembered. My heart remembered because those words, whispered in childhood evenings, never failed to carry us swiftly away to another land.

> The beauty of the world hath made me sad,
> This beauty that will pass;
> Sometimes my heart hath shaken with great joy
> To see a leaping squirrel in a tree,
> Or a red lady-bird upon a stalk,
> Or little rabbits in a field at evening,
> Lit by a slanting sun,
> Or some green hill where shadows drifted by
> Some quiet hill where mountain man hath sown
> And soon would reap; near to the gate of heaven;
> Or children with bare feet upon the sands
> Of some ebbed sea, or playing on the streets
> Of little towns in Connacht;
> Things young and happy.
> And then my heart hath told me:
> These will pass,
> Will pass and change, will die and be no more,
> Things bright and green, things young and happy;

And I have gone upon my way
Sorrowful.[1]

The Wounded Child

But there are other wounds that must be healed. Eric Fromm points to three kinds of wounds, three kinds of alienation that punish the soul and stifle its growth: alienation from the inner self, from the human community and from the cosmos. The latter divisions are reflected upon throughout this book, e.g. in The Creative Heart, The Erotic Heart and The Eucharistic Heart. These wounds must be healed before the divine life-forces can bless our days with Love's own wisdom and joy. The gifts of spontaneity, vitality and creativity have their sources inside and outside us. When the flow of power is cut, so too is inspiration and imagination and compassion. The depression that follows upon alienation makes it impossible to be truly human. I wish to reflect here on the wounded child within each of us—the consequence of our alienation from our true self.

I often wonder if there may not be sinister reasons for our reluctance to become more knowledgeable about the phenomenon of the wounded child in all of us and the incalculable distortion, destruction, despair and deep suffering that ensue in so very many instances. Adult depression is almost always linked with the wounds of childhood. And until these wounds are healed the adult is not free to experience consciously certain feelings or to be present to emotions of all kinds in an appropriately spontaneous manner. When the wounded child inside is dumb, so is the adult artist. Because to create, one must feel. And to truly feel there must be a condition of simplicity and a harmony of energies. Why is the child within so wounded and why is that child estranged?

Most of us can only guess at the intensity of the child's desire to please the parents. A child has no choice here. It is a necessity. Because parents are not perfect, each carrying his or her own wounded child—often quite unconsciously— within, there is much exploitation and manipulation going on. On the one hand there is the parent with needs for power and control, and sometimes with very unrealistic expectations regarding the perfect child. On the other hand, the child, as we mentioned, is committed, at all costs, to the pursuit of pleasing the parent. (In many cases, especially when the child is very young, the mother is central.) When what comes naturally to the child is met with horror, disgust or even disapproval by the mother, the child swiftly learns to adjust and adapt and pretend. This pretense leads to the "as-if" syndrome and the false self begins to grow and eventually take over. The child has sensed the absence of unconditional love and, at the awful expense of integrity and truth, contrives to become, at any cost, the object of love in the eyes of the parents. That is why the unfolding of an authentic emotional life is prevented in its infancy and the otherwise ever-green well springs of vitality and creativity remain blocked off for decades and very often for ever. It is important to spell out the results of recent research in this field a little more fully.

The parents have found in their child's "false self" the confirmation they were looking for, a substitute for their own missing structures; the child, who has been unable to build up his own structures, is first consciously and unconsciously (through the introject) dependent on his parents. He cannot rely on his own emotions, has not come to experience them through trial and error, has no sense of his own real needs, and is alienated from himself to the highest degree. Under these circumstances he cannot separate from his parents, and even as an adult he is still dependent on affirmation from his partner, from groups and especially from his own children. The heirs of the parents are the introjectors (children) from whom the "true self" must remain concealed, and so loneliness in the parental home is later followed by isolation within the self. Narcissistic cathexis of her child by the mother does not exclude emotional devotion.[2]

All this is rather alarming and disturbing. The child is certainly loved but as a "self-object," excessively and not in the way the child needs and always on the condition that the child presents the false self. Even though the child cannot see through the unconscious manipulation of the parent, since it is like the air that is breathed in without the possibility of an alternative, nevertheless the seeds of a tragedy are being sown. To avoid losing the parent's object-love, there is the compulsion to gratify the parent's unconscious needs at the cost of the child's self-realization. The child is forced to violate its own innate sense of truth and justice. This was the cost of "earned love"—the sacrifice of self. Otherwise the fear would be too great. Hermann Hesse wrote in "A Child's Heart,"

If I were to reduce all my feelings and their painful conflicts to a single name, I can think of no other word but "dread." It was dread—dread and uncertainty—that I felt in all those hours of shattered childhood felicity; dread of punishment, dread of my own conscience, dread of stirrings in my soul which I considered forbidden and criminal.[3]

These are heart breaking stories. And we think they are about others.

Decades later, maybe in mid-life, by one means or another, many tormented souls begin the arduous journey backward to reclaim their lost selves from a plundered childhood. They are driven to undertake this daunting task by the intensity of their self-hatred, self-contempt, deep anger, and loss of inspiration, spontaneity and creativity. A deepening depression trickles and then flows into every nook and cranny of the psyche. This dark depression, as so many only too well are aware, takes the light out of life. "The true opposite of depression," writes Alice Miller, "is not gaiety or absence of pain, but vitality; the freedom to experience spontaneous feelings."[4] This depression, later understood as arising from a subconscious reaction to the loss of self or alienation from self, is often experienced as emptiness, futility, fear and loneliness. There is no self-esteem because there is no authenticity of one's own feeling of worth or pride. There is only a denial of basic emotions and feelings—a denial which began many decades before. ". . . there are children who have not been free to experience the very earliest feelings such as discontent, anger, rage, pain, even hunger and, of course, enjoyment of their own bodies."[5]

Storms of rage may shake the soul of the prisoner of childhood when these truths emerge. The violence of the profound indignation at the humiliation of the defenseless infant whose identity was commandeered by pirate-parents is often expressed in the most physically and verbally explosive fashion.[6] But all this is, believe it or not, good news. The journey has begun. It is not the nature of the feelings that are here expressed that is important, but the very fact that feelings are being expressed. There is a temptation to think that if we *conceptually* apprehend the history of our slow or stunted or non-development, we are making headway. Maybe. It is better than the absence of feeling. But it must be emphasized that it is the EXPERIENCE of emotion that unlocks the door of our dark and shuttered heart.

And then the mourning begins. The heart weeps for a lost child. The spirit grieves for a young will broken, a young pride humiliated, a young hope ridiculed, a young beauty defiled, a young, complete *person* disrespected, a childhood irretrievably looted. The mourning may take a long time, but the part of the true self that somehow survived (in torment) begins to possess its own truth again—a truth that was despised and devalued, rejected, suppressed (and sometimes almost totally destroyed) for too long. Slowly the outrage subsides; the false self is let go; the mourning brings relief; the healing begins to happen. The human spirit is indeed indomitable. To achieve what I have just outlined usually supposes a long, lonely and bloody struggle. But our beautiful souls will not lie down and die. While there is breath in the body the spirit is indestructible. Given half a chance, life will always win.

All these truths our heart is teaching us. We have learned that the child is the mother of the adult and must emerge within us as a divine messenger carrying secrets about a real and forgotten world—a world that sent her son into the vineyard of this planet, all unsuspecting of the awful fate to be meted out by those who were trusted most. We learned that we pursue a peculiar if not poisonous pedagogy when we force children to obey so that we can teach them about love. We do not have to educate children to be good or to be just. We don't have to train children to forgive as we do. We pray that one day we may learn to forgive as freely as they do. Because they are already the small prophets of great gods. We have learned that before the true self can grow again, the wounded child must be healed by mourning, when our bleeding sores are revealed and our pain is unmasked and the self is finally accepted. We have learned that no one is to blame and that this realization is vital in the second soul-making of a hurt but quickening spirit. No one is to blame, because our parents too were wounded children, a woundedness often transcended by the extravagance of their love.

And then, on the edge of this moment, we have learned

that we can see into the land where Spring always comes and where compassion, wisdom and power impatiently wait to bless and grace the dry and shrunken lives of each refugee from the many prison camps of childhood. It is also at this brink, where light and darkness meet, where trust and fear embrace, where life and death do their timeless dance that our resilient hearts become creative again and beat out a new tempo for laughing feet.

The Healing

During the days of the writing of this chapter there have been many brutal murders in the North of Ireland. One hour ago I took a break to watch the news. I will never forget what I saw. There was a crazed look of violence on the faces of my countryfolk as they obscenely beat two men to death earlier today on the streets of Belfast. There was madness and fear in the unearthly screaming of the mob as it hacked to pieces, stripped and then repeatedly shot their fellow humans in another devilish moment of our shameful history. The nausea that enveloped me arose from my sense of identity with the murdered men and also with the blood-lusting attackers. The terrifying aspect of the explosion of hatred was that they were all "ordinary" people, from "ordinary" homes, attending a funeral in a city in Western Europe in 1988.

From where does it come, this awful curse of hatred that blights the precious plants of growing youth? And for those for whom age has brought no wisdom, where is the love that held them close in their defenseless years? The raw wounds of alienation were torn open again today with a ferocity that defies explanation. There is a desperate helplessness in human hearts tonight—because the evil we see in others is, we know, alive and well within ourselves (cf. The Dark Heart). And so we search for hope and light. The only reasons for living are those we find in the hearts of people who love even more in the face of hatred and evil, who redouble their efforts to remain open, to unify and to keep "letting go." All three flow out from a compassionate heart. This we learn from Love herself. For the Christian it is epitomized in Jesus Christ; before him it was the blueprint of the opening action of creation. God's flowing out is a divine letting go into a unifying openness. This is Love's vulnerable way of incarnation. It is why God suffers. It is the reason why we still hope.

At the end of time billions of people were scattered on a great plain before God's dwelling. Most avoided the brilliance before them, but some groups near the front talked heatedly—not in fear but with aggression. These were disillusioned men and women for whom the struggle against evil and human brutality had been too much. There was no reason left to hope.

"Why should we believe anymore? Anyway, what does God know about pain?" snapped a pert young brunette. She ripped open a sleeve to reveal a tattooed number from a Nazi concentration camp. "We endured, terror, beatings, torture, death. . . ."

In another group a Negro boy lowered his collar. "What about this?" he demanded, showing an ugly rope burn. "Lynched for no crime but being black."

In another bitter group was a one-parent schoolgirl with sullen eyes. "Why should I have had to suffer?" she rapped out. "It wasn't my fault."

I noticed there one of the young men whose awful death I had just witnessed on television. His voice shook with anger as he described his death. Dragged from his companions, he was beaten, stripped, mutilated by a frenzied mob, and finally murdered. "My naked body was suspended from a wall above the jeering people," he shouted, "and they danced on my clothes. Where were you then? It wouldn't have happened to you!"

Far out across the plains were hundreds of such groups. Each had a complaint against God for the evil and suffering running wild in the world. God was beyond all this where neither fears nor tears, hunger or hatred darkened the heavenly hearts.

So each of these groups sent forth their leader—the one who had suffered the most.

A Jew, a black person, a citizen of Hiroshima, an African slave, a white witch, a thalidomide child, an AIDS victim, a mid-Eastern freedom-fighter . . . In the center of the plain they consulted together. At last they were ready to present their case. It was rather clever.

Before God could be qualified to be their God, their hope, especially their judge, all that they had endured must be endured by that same God. They called on God to live on earth as a human being.

Let him be born a Jew. Let the legitimacy of his birth be doubted.

Give her a task so difficult that even her own family will think her crazy.

Let him be betrayed by closest friends.

Let her face false charges, be tried by a prejudiced jury, and convicted by a partisan judge.

Let him be beaten, tortured, stripped, killed, raised aloft and jeered at by people like himself.

At the end let her know what it is like to be utterly and terribly alone.

At the moment of death let him experience total despair.

When the last had finished outlining the context of this incarnation there was a long silence.

Nobody uttered another word.

Nobody moved.

Something had occurred to them . . .

Meister Eckhart puts it better than most. "Jesus became a human being because God, the compassionate one, could not suffer and lacked a back to be beaten. God needed a back like

ours on which to receive blows and thereby to perform compassion as well as to preach it. However great one's suffering
is, if it comes through God, God suffers from it first."[7]

Living the Mystery

When it comes to pain, we can but live the questions—and
trust.

As to your own individual suffering, being human, you'd naturally
try to avoid pain and would reasonably dread any form of imminent
agony. Yet, in retrospect, if your life had been devoid of all pain,
you could be said to have missed much of life's richest experience.
For pain often includes a goodly component of soul satisfaction and
it surely has spiritual meaning. Also, impossible as it would be to
prove it in this mortal phase of transcendence, pain may well, in
fact, be the greatest language of the soul.[8]

Since it appears that there are no answers to hand, in the face
of this divine mystery, what are the questions? Is there something so precious about pure Love that when incarnated into
time and space it can only emerge as suffering? Are there
places in the heart that do not yet exist and into them we enter
suffering so that they may have existence? Is pain and
woundedness a consequent of vision, as with Teilhard de
Chardin when he wept at the distance between the way things
were and the way they ought to be? Or is suffering the cause
of wisdom and vision as Elgar hoped when he remarked
about a very gifted singer, "She will be really great when
something happens to break her heart"?

Once upon a time in the heart of the Western Kingdom lay a beautiful garden. And there in the cool of the day the Master of the Garden

liked to walk. Of all the creatures of the garden, the most beautiful and most beloved was a gracious and noble bamboo tree. Year after year Bamboo grew yet more noble and gracious, conscious of her Master's love and watchful delight, but always modest and gentle.

And often, when the wind came to revel, in the garden, Bamboo would cast aside her grave stateliness to dance and play merrily, tossing and swaying and leaping and bowing in joyous abandon, leading the Great Dance of the Garden, which delighted the Master's heart.

Now one day the Master sat down to contemplate his Bamboo with eyes of curious expectancy. Bamboo, in a passion of adoration, bowed her great head to the ground in loving greeting. The Master spoke: "Bamboo, I would use you."

Bamboo flung her head to the sky in utter delight. The day of days had come, the day for which she had been made, the day to which she had been growing, hour by hour, the day in which she would find her completion and her destiny. Her voice came softly: "Master, I am ready. Use me as you will."

"Bamboo"—the Master's voice was grave, "I would like to take you and—cut you down!"

"Cut . . . me . . . down! Me . . . whom you, Master, had made the most beautiful in all your garden . . . cut me down! Not that, not that. Use me for your joy, O Master, but do not cut me down!"

"Beloved Bamboo"—the Master's voice grew graver still—"if I do not cut you down, I cannot use you."

The garden grew still . . . Wind held his breath. Bamboo slowly bent her proud and glorious head. Then came a whisper: "Master, if you cannot use me unless you cut me down . . . then . . . do *your* will and cut."

"Bamboo, beloved Bamboo, I need to cut your leaves and branches from you also."

"Master, Master, please spare me. Cut me down and lay my beauty in the dust, but would you also take from me my leaves and branches?"

"Bamboo, if I do not cut them away, I cannot use you."

The sun hid his face. A listening butterfly glided fearfully away. And Bamboo shivered in terrible expectancy, whispering low, "Master, cut away."

"Bamboo, Bamboo, I would also split you in two and cut out your heart, for if I don't I cannot use you."

Then was Bamboo bowed to the ground. "Master, Master . . . then cut me and split me."

So did the Master of the Garden take Bamboo and cut her down and hacked off her branches and stripped off her leaves and cleaved her in two and cut out her heart. And lifting her gently, he carried her to where there was a spring of fresh, sparkling water in the midst of his dry fields. Then putting one end of broken Bamboo into the spring and the other end into the water channel in his field, the Master laid down gently his beloved Bamboo. The clear sparkling waters raced joyously down the channel of Bamboo's torn body into the waiting fields. Then the rice was planted and the days went by, and the shoots grew and the harvest came.

In that day was Bamboo, once so glorious in her stately beauty, yet more glorious in her brokenness and humility. For in her beauty she was life abundant, but in her brokenness she became a channel of abundant life to her Master's world.

NOTES

1. Padraig Pearce, *Plays, Stories, Poems* (Dublin: Talbot Press, 1963 reprint) p. 341. (Pearce was an Irish mystic, poet, freedom-fighter who was executed by the British forces for his inspiration of the Easter Monday Uprising, 1916.)

2. Alice Miller, *The Drama of the Gifted Child* (New York: Basic Books, 1981) p. 14.

3. Hermann Hesse, "A Child's Heart," in *Klingsor's Last Summer* (New York: Harper and Row, 1971) p. 10; quoted in Miller p. 96.

4. Miller, p. 57.

5. Ibid. p. 46.

6. Bob Hoffman, *No One Is To Blame* (Palo Alto, CA: E.P. Dutton and Co., 1979) cf. ch. 5.

7. Matthew Fox, *Meditations with Meister Eckhart,* (Santa Fe: Bear and Co., 1983) pp. 100–101.

8. Guy Murchie, *The Seven Mysteries of Life* (Boston: Houghton Mifflin Co., 1978) pp. 518–519.

HEART'S SPRING

A Time for Creating

&

I have learned that "youthfulness," creativity and divinity are intrinsically inter-connected. Meister Eckhart sees God as eternally young and giving birth unceasingly. We too stay young when the original vision of the child at play in us continues to charm us through the decades. It is this same child, repeatedly healed from its wounds, that plays forever in the cosmos first and then in heaven.

MARCH

The Young Heart

"Heavens, how you've aged!"
exclaimed the Master after
speaking with a boyhood friend.

"One cannot help growing old,
can one?" said the friend.

"No, one cannot," agreed the
Master, "but one must avoid
becoming aged."
—ANTHONY DE MELLO

Only the century of the child has made us study childhood and indeed
youth, not only as causal precursors of adulthood as it was and is, but
also as a potential promise for what adulthood may yet become.
—ERIK ERIKSON

The Young Heart

Some words from the sermons of the perennial mystic, Meister Eckhart, will lead us happily into this section.

When we say, "God is eternal," we mean: God is eternally young. God is ever green, ever verdant, ever flowering. Every action of God is new, for he makes all things new. God is the newest thing there is; the youngest thing there is. God is the beginning and if we are united with him we become new again. [1]

Newness, youth and a sense of the "eternal now"—there are those whose hearts have never lost these precious qualities of life, who have not outlived their childhood and have grown as a tree grows, ever more itself as the seasons circle round it, realizing its true nature and establishing this nature forever. In such a way of growing, time is redeemed. The child does not gradually develop adulthood. As life unfolds the child simply realizes what he/she already is. The fullness is there from the beginning; it is not acquired by stages. There is a fine balance here at the intersection of time and timelessness.

Christianity is aware of the mystery of that beginning which already contains all present within itself, and yet still has to become all; the beginning which is the basis and foundation of all that is yet to come, its horizon and its law, and yet at the same time cannot ever come to its own fullness except in what has still to come in the future. [2]

When growing is regarded from a linear perspective according to the laws of physical time where the past is lost and the present is a stepping-stone to the future, the young heart begins to age and forget. When that for which childhood is a preparation arrives, childhood itself disappears. The child is more than a potential adult who will one day arrive at its ultimate goal, having passed through the stages of earlier years as definitively and irrevocably as one passes through the stations on a railway journey en route to one's final destination.

But the heart of the child, like that of the lover and the poet, cannot be evaluated in such a way and does not fit on an assembly-line or on a grid of stage-development theory. Because a child is mystery, he/she is outside total assessment. There is an eternal quality about a child's heart. Childhood is not lived through and cast away like an old coat. It endures as the fullness of the person. We grow out of our childishness with its sulks and its tantrums, its demands and its false expectations. But we do not lose childhood. It may well be a wounded childhood, and to this topic of supreme importance we have turned our attention already in "The Wounded Heart." But childhood itself is not discarded. Rather, we affirm it and in a sense

we only become the children we were because we gather up time—and in this our childhood too—into our eternity. . . . We do not move away from childhood in any definitive sense, but rather move toward the eternity of this childhood, to its definitive and enduring validity in God's sight. . . . It is important in itself also, as a stage of humanity's personal history in which that takes place which can only take place in childhood itself, a field which bears fair flowers and ripe fruits such as can grow in *this* field and in no other, and which will themselves be carried into the storehouses of eternity.[3]

About seven hundred years before Karl Rahner, another poet of the Word, in equally striking but simpler words wrote:

My soul is as young as the day it was created. Yes, and much younger. In fact I am younger today than I was yesterday, and if I am not younger tomorrow than I was yesterday I would be ashamed of myself. People who dwell in God dwell in the eternal now. There, people can never grow old. There, everything is present and everything is new.[4]

Every time I fling a small child into the air (the equivalent of my being thrown about thirty feet high), I marvel at her trust and unquestioning dependence as she squeals with exhilaration and fearful delight. I chose to offer my reflections on "the young heart," in this section, in terms of the qualities of true childhood. Childhood as an inherent factor in our lives must take the form of trust, of openness, of expectation, of readiness to be controlled by another, of interior harmony with the unpredictable forces with which the individual finds himself/herself confronted. There are other graces that we identify in the eternal child. There is a quality of freedom, there is an innocent receptivity and an unclouded hope, there is a natural delight in play. The young heart possesses a native sense of wonder—the awareness that things are, which precedes the investigation and analysis of what they are. Perhaps above all, the hallmark of the young heart is its capacity for open and direct relationships. To this radical combination of simple and unqualified openness and potential for growth and becoming (eventually as full participants in the Godhead) I now turn.

Eckhart speaks of God in terms of openness, youthfulness, freshness and newness. Because all people are created in God's image such seeds of Love's essence are sown in every young heart. It is only in terms of these insights and revelations that we begin to make sense of the mysterious "eternal now" that keeps a heart young. "God so created all things that he nevertheless always creates in the present. The act of creation does not fade into the past but is always in the beginning and in process and new."⁵ When in youthful openness the human soul meets and melts with the Love which gave it birth, then finite time collapses into the "eternal now." And then, as Matthew Fox puts it, for those who are ready all has been prepared. Present and new in a timeless vision is the intimation of all that is, or was, or will be—a moment out of time but one that is never forgotten by the open heart held in vigilant readiness by unendingly "letting go." Examples abound of what the nature of such timeless visions might be. Some experiences are for a moment; others, of less intensity perhaps, continue for some time. I have already alluded to some accounts of these mystical interludes in "The Wondering Heart."

What follows is a description of a childhood moment of disclosure which happened in Pangbourne, Berkshire, England, during an evening walk on the moors some decades ago. It is well researched and carefully presented. I take up the story toward the end.

. . . Suddenly I seemed to see the mist as a shimmering gossamer tissue and the harebells, appearing here and there, seemed to shine with a brilliant fire. Somehow I understood that this was the living tissue of life itself, in which that which we call consciousness was embedded, appearing here and there as a shining focus of energy in the more diffused whole. In that moment I knew that I had my special place, as had all other things animate and inanimate, and that we were all part of this universal tissue which was both fragile yet immensely strong, and utterly good and beneficent.

The vision has never left me. It is as clear today as fifty years ago, and with it the same intense feeling of love of the world and the certainty of ultimate good. It gave me then a strong, clear sense of identity which has withstood many vicissitudes, and an affinity with plants, birds, animals, even insects, and people too, which has often been commented upon. Moreover, the whole of this experience has since formed a kind of reservoir of strength fed from an unseen source, from which quite suddenly in the midst of the very darkest times a bubble of pure joy rises through it all, and I know that whatever the anguish, there is some deep centre in my life which cannot be touched by it . . . the point is that by whatever mysterious perception, the whole impression and its total meaning were apprehended in a single instant. Years later, reading Traherne and Meister Eckhart and Francis of Assisi, I have cried aloud with surprise and joy, knowing myself to be in the company of others who had shared the same kind of experience and who had been able to set it down marvellously. This is not the only experience of its kind that has occurred to me—indeed these occur relatively often. . . .[6]

To have visions and dreams, to live in the "eternal now," to have a heart at play, in freedom and in wonder and in openness, to know the rich emptiness of a heart familiar with "letting go"—may you experience all these blessings in your heart forever young.

Prayer of Awareness

We often yearn for our lost childhood, sometimes deeply and sometimes bitterly. The original vision we have discussed so often belongs to people's childhood. Somewhere along the way, the unity intrinsic to the integrated personality becomes radically fragmented. The effects of such separation and alienation are devastating. We are shipwrecked in space, dying for want of our homeland oxygen. This book is about identifying the distances between what has gone adrift and about suggesting connections to bring about a life-giving bonding.

As I reflected on these truths I found that I longed for a more intimate sense of belonging within my self, with my body, with the environment and the cosmos, and with the hearts of my friends. It was a strange kind of loneliness that I felt as when you hear a distant faint call that is unidentifiable yet stirs something within. And the Spirit was only too ready to help me . . . It was a bright December morning when my friend Tony and I walked across the Interstate Line between Nevada and North California along the shores of Lake Tahoe. I deciphered four movements in my stream of consciousness. I first became deeply aware of my body and its movements beneath my warm and glowing skin. I spoke to its many parts assuring them of my love and requesting forgiveness for the abuses and carelessness of the past. I began with my heart, my very center, the focus of life and love. I told my heart I was in wonder at its power. To keep the trunk-artery busy, the heart's daily work is

equivalent to lifting a ton from the ground up to the top of a five-story building and in a lifetime may beat four billion times . . . each time squeezing, twisting and literally wringing the blood out of itself with four complex sets of spiral muscles triggered by a kind of electrical timer that is directly connected with the brain, while its rubbery one-way valves automatically flap, click and rest with their familiar song of lubb-dup, lubb-dup, lubb-dup just beneath the front ribs.[7]

I became aware of the times I have abused my liver with alcohol and my lungs with cigarettes. I acknowledged the muscles of my body and how well they have served me. I thanked my faithful legs that never once let me down, carrying me trustingly through my agonies and ecstasies, my sins and visions, my victories and failures in my half-century pilgrimage on this planet. How strange that I have not seriously praised my eyes before—those miracles of creation in all their delicate perfection. Could I live without the shapes and colors of this world and the fragile beauty of the lovely faces that fill my days? I felt at one with my senses then, and addressed them in turn: my ears, my tongue, my hands—how resilient they are in protecting themselves and in taking care of me! So much pleasure, joy and wonder they have brought and how little I have appreciated their devotion! I continued to visit my body for another few minutes and then became aware once again of the magnificent surroundings whose guest I was that morning. Strengthened by the unity that reconciliation with my body had brought I then became sensitive to the impatient and loving energy of the environment in particular and the cosmos in general, waiting to empower me with their mighty spirit.

After some silence, broken only by the steady beat of hearts and feet (Tony and I had now begun to jog), we entered into another litany of praise and thanks, this time a dialogue with nature and the elements of the environment. We imagined that the center of our power was high in our bellies, right behind the navel, and that here was the locus of the energies of our lives. As our feet rhythmically touched the earth, the forces of the universe were streaming through our legs with currents of power straight from the heart of the earth. We thanked this sturdy planet for its perennial support and knew instinctively that it loved us.

As though the tops of our heads were open like small chimneys, we imagined the creative energy of the sun gracing us with its vitality and striking through us to meet and mingle with its sister-power at the center of our being. These mighty forces joined in an irresistible bond to pulse their relentless way through the veins, muscles and fibers of our bodies and then, with playful joy, their job well done, they rushed back to join the cosmic heart from which they came and start all over again. A new awareness flowed over us, of being held gently at the nurturing breasts of our newly discovered and compassionate mother. It was such a good feeling, one of recognition and arrival, like knowing you are safe in the right place at the right time.

And then a kind of silent music was felt. The trees, like long-lost cousins, offered us their still and silent strength. The rocks, delighted with themselves that morning for some reason, gleefully motioned us on and then, just as we laughingly acknowledged their support, we rounded a bend to behold, in huge letters on a flat-faced elderly boulder, the word "ENJOY." Moved by such synchronicity we knew again a free-flowing oneness with all of nature and rejoiced as we felt the call of the shimmering water-colored lake in the distance below us calling to its sister-water that fills our bodies at all times. And so, as with the various body-parts a little earlier, we spoke to, thanked and praised—and in so doing we worshiped—in turn, the grass, the air, the clouds, the frost, our shadows, and the myriads of flora and fauna that teemed with excited life around us.

After meditating in silence for a while on our sudden and wondrous encounters with these new and alluring relations, we set our attention toward opening a third set of life-giving and precious sources—the font and spring of yet another love, this time flowing from the human hearts of those who love us and who grace and bless the days and nights and seasons of our lives. We shared reflections on the immense force of these waves of human love that flood our fragile spirit with hope and courage. We noticed the strange resistance we often offer to the unconditional love of those amazing lovers who love us in that way. And we wondered at that. We prayed then for a divine openness and vulnerability so that the hearts of those who are bestowing upon us the greatest gift of all would merge with ours in an explosion of pure power.

Here we felt was the center of our cosmic interconnectedness. We moved toward this holy space and knew

it to be so. Willingly caught in the center of the web, we felt
suspended by the network of touching hearts across land and
oceans. We were in a world now of distilled energy. Very
clearly I relived the wars of my love in the past, the dark and
bloody battles of bitter misunderstanding, the hard hacking
at the unyielding rock-face of jealousy, the healing balm of
final forgiveness, the deep and rich love that now blessed all
my moments. We prayed then to the Mysterious Spirit to
forgive us for our unprecedented slaughter of innocent life as
we exploit, manipulate and destroy the environment and all
non-human life, ourselves and each other. The cries of our
sisters and brothers in their unnecessary torment rolled like
angry thunder over the hills and across the valleys and lake
that morning.

To be reconciled; to be forgiven. It would take a long time.
We felt responsible for the cosmos and we prayed with St.
Francis:

> Lord, make me an instrument of your peace;
> Where there is hatred, let me sow your love;
> Where there is injury, pardon;
> Where there is doubt, faith;
> Where there is despair, hope;
> Where there is darkness, light;
> And where there is sadness, joy . . .

We both felt a desire to be at one with the universe, to be
an intrinsic part of all creation. As we drove quietly home, I
shared this Buddhist story with Tony.

A doll of salt, after a long pilgrimage on dry land, came to
the sea and discovered something she had never seen and
could not possibly understand. She stood on the firm ground,
a solid little doll of salt, and saw that there was another
ground that was mobile, insecure, noisy, strange and un-

known. She asked the sea, "But what *are* you?" The sea answered, "Touch me." So the doll shyly put forward a foot and touched the water and she got a strange impression that it was something that began to be knowable. She withdrew her leg, looked and saw that her toe had gone. She was afraid and asked, "Oh where is my toe, what have you done to me?" And the sea said, "You have given something in order to understand."

Gradually the water took away small bits of the doll's salt and the doll went further and further into the sea, and at every moment she had a sense of understanding more and more, and yet of not being able to say what the sea was. As she went deeper she melted more and more, repeating, "But what is the sea?" At last a wave dissolved the rest of her and the doll said, "It is I." She had discovered what the sea was, but not yet what the water was.

NOTES

1. Matthew Fox, *Meditations with Meister Eckhart* (Santa Fe: Bear and Co., 1983) p. 32.

2. Karl Rahner, *Theological Investigations,* Vol. 3 (London: Darton, Longman and Todd, 1971) p. 34.

3. Ibid. p. 35.

4. Fox, p. 32.

5. Matthew Fox, *Breakthrough: Meister Eckhart's Creation Spirituality in New Translation* (New York: Image Books, 1980) p. 113.

6. Edward Robinson, *The Original Vision* (Oxford: Religious Experience Research Unit, 1977) p. 33.

7. Guy Murchie, *The Seven Mysteries of Life* (Boston: Houghton Mifflin, 1978) p. 121.

APRIL

The Green Heart

If you keep a green bough
in your heart
the singing bird
will come
—Chinese Proverb

In the beginning all creatures were green and vital;
they flourished amidst flowers.
Later the green figure itself
came down.
—Hildegard of Bingen

The Green Heart

The Regional Trail between Lafayette and Moraga stretches through the undulating and beautiful Contra Costa country-side near the San Francisco Bay area. On a sun-drenched mid-day in early Spring I was padding along on my daily jog trying to get a handle on my homework for Shanja, my teacher. "Express in images and words," she said, "the most important moments of your life—by next Monday!" Over the previous days I had wrestled with poems and pictures to no avail. And then, like a warm breeze in late evening, my heart told me this story. It is a story about a stained-glass window.

Small Wonder

How I loved being young and new. It was like one long childhood morning.

> . . . it was all
> Shining; it was Adam and maiden
> So it must have been after the birth of
> the simple light
> In the first spinning place . . .[1]

My colors sang. I was beautiful. My shapes, all day, made love with their shadows. My world was a playground. Every move was made in adventure. Every breath was drawn in excitement. There was only magic.

> Now as I was young and easy under
> the apple boughs
> About the lilting house and happy

> as the grass was green,
> The night above the dingle starry,
> Time let me hail and climb
> Golden in the heydays of his eyes,
> And honoured among wagons, I was
> prince of the apple towns
> And once below a time I lordly had the trees and leaves
> Trail with daisies and barley
> Down the rivers of the windfall light.[2]

I understood everything without knowing. I felt everything without being taught. I was a prince in my kingdom of joy.

> And honoured among foxes and pheasants by the gay house
> Under the new made clouds and happy as the heart was long,
> In the sun born over and over,
> I ran my heedless ways . . .
> Nothing I cared, in the lamb white days . . .[3]

The earth ached for the touch of my bare feet and begged the sun to warm it early (for me) each Spring. When the wind blew we danced to rhythms felt. The yearning waters of the Summer streams played havoc with my heart. And in the fires of night-time I traveled eternities. I think I was always laughing then.

> All the sun long it was running, it was lovely.
> The hay-fields high as the house,
> the tunes from the chimneys,
> it was air and playing,
> lovely and watery
> and fire green as grass.
> And the Sabbath rang slowly
> in the pebbles of the holy streams . . .[4]

I was the world and the world was me and the world would never end. Not while the sun shone. Because the sun was my soul. Without me the sun had no meaning. Without the sun I was dead. Oh how we loved. All day long. And how, each night, I could hardly wait for my love to come. And she never missed a morning. Then she would play wild with my beauty. Without a sound she would call forth my deepest treasures and every moment was full. We lived together in a mystery of light and color as we co-created an ever-changing radiance for the dancing galaxies and the bopping grasshoppers.

We were famous. Because we were perfect. We were perfect because we were always changing. We had to. Sister sun was always moving, always new. And so I was always different in ever-fresh combinations of my colors. People were amazed. They came from all over. And we played tricks on their faces making old people young again and healing small babies who had grown too silent.

At my center was a perfect heart. When the sun shone, that heart was only power and light.

Lost Light

Without warning winter came. How dark it is when the light goes out—darker by far than if it had never shone, and darker still for one who had become the light. From what caverns of dark mystery came this deadly guest of my soul? Was it within myself—or somewhere else? Could this be true? Why did it happen? When did it begin? How was I deceived? Only yesterday, together, we had charmed the world—today I was nothing.

I had, in truth, noticed the ivy. So weak and soft it crept below and whispered up its plea for one small space—a space

to be. Oh I was young then and very much in love and our
brilliant heart was greening the world. If I had a place for my
feet I could have juggled with the planets. It was early Spring
and the tender plant, no longer just lying against me, was
creeping and spreading silently and quietly. Clinging and
sticky now like its offshoots, I confess to a sense of strong
uneasiness whenever I paused from my intense allurements.
But I was proud and strong then, empowered by the very
spirit of the sun herself, our lives racing with the shadows
filling each empty space in tune with the mighty turning of
the faithful earth.

This night would be a long one. In fact I thought it would
never end. Coiling around me like a frightened snake the ivy,
once so tender and supple, was now hard and thick. Crushed
and strangled I choked for breath and, like the small ivy of that
fateful Spring, I whispered for help. How weak the strongest is
and how vulnerable the most secure! How brief the days of
wild play and how fragile the gentle love-affair of light and
color! My sun had set; my light was out; my colors dead. In
splinters all around me lay the jagged memories of the infinite
creativity I once was. The shattered glass of my broken beauty
brought spiraling memories of descending despair.

Had I not been attentive to my soul? Or had I taken the
light for granted? Was there no service in my love, no sacrifice in my worship?

My lifeless thoughts were bitter. In the empty and dark
silence of nothingness I tasted death for the first time and a
cold fear gripped my once-bright heart. It was at that moment I noticed her. She was about seven and she had a front
tooth missing. To correct her right-eye sight there was a
cardboard patch covering half her spectacles. One of God's
special playmates, she clearly lived in a world of her own,
speaking a language that only the angels could understand. A
sign of contradiction, she witnessed forever to the difference

that God is. She was now playing with a ray of sunlight, reaching on tiptoe to catch it on her face. With sudden astonishment I realized that I was not all-dark, all-empty, all-dead. The pencil of pale light that shimmered on the innocent grinning face was heart-shaped. Even though it had lost its power my heart had held its shape and my sister sun had found the one open space in my whole being. With the accuracy of love it had penetrated my center, carrying a tiny remnant of my former power to create a new smile—the special attribute of God herself—on the face of Love's own young image.

Like the sudden easing of throbbing pain or the end of a crippling fear the beginning of hope stirred somewhere within me. But it would be a long journey and a slow dawn.

Slow Dawn

How well I remember the graced days that followed my encounter with the wounded child. I began to see my own brokenness, wounds and sense of loss in this new and healing light. But the dawn came slowly between the sun and the ivy, between the light and the shadow. I remember a conversation with the ivy as a moment of blessing. "I am, you see," she said, "your shadow," and she went on to explain that as well as possessing the qualities that almost killed my heart, she also protected so much of the undeveloped parts of me—the diamonds in the rough, so to speak. If I could embrace her, pay attention to her, accept her into my being there would be gifts and insights and wisdom far outweighing the talents and powers of my earlier days. To make her point, she told me then a story.

Each day the king sat in state hearing petitions and dispensing justice. Each day a holy man, dressed in the robe of an ascetic beggar approached the king and without a word offered him a piece of very ripe fruit. Each day the king accepted the "present" from the beggar and without a thought handed it to his treasurer who stood behind the throne. Each day the beggar, again without a word, withdrew and vanished into the crowd.

Year after year this precise same ritual occurred every day the king sat in office. Then one day, some 10 years after the holy man first appeared, something different happened. A tame monkey, having escaped from the women's apartments in the inner palace, came bounding into the hall and leaped upon the arm of the king's throne. The ascetic beggar had just presented the king with his usual gift of fruit, but this time instead of passing it on to his treasurer as was his usual custom, the king handed it over to the monkey. When the animal bit into it, a precious jewel dropped out and fell to the floor.

The king was amazed and quickly turned to his treasurer behind him. "What has become of all the others?" he asked. But the treasurer had no answer. Over all the years he had simply thrown the unimpressive "gifts" through a small upper window in the treasure house, not even bothering to unlock the door. So he excused himself and ran quickly to the vault. He opened it and hurried to the area beneath the little window. There, on the floor, lay a mass of rotten fruit in various stages of decay. But amidst this garbage of many years lay a heap of precious gems.[5]

We spoke about the story for a long time and we reflected on our relationship during the decades of dark diminishment. "I am a precious part of you," she said, "and you need me to bring you to wholeness and completion." She explained to me that I was refusing to grow; that I *thought* I was changing but was not really letting go; that I lacked the courage to face the fact that what I once thought of as "wrong" or "right" may no longer be so; that I had rejected much of my "anima," the feminine counterpart of my masculine persona. The ivy, my shadow, was the substance of all of these and much more. She was the wounded child in need of nurture and reconciliation; she was the frustration and suppression that was strangling my creativity; she was the deep resentment and guilt that twisted around my psyche as strands of arrogance, laziness, anger and sometimes evil. Slowly I began to realize that I was not in control of my life; that I had identified with my many addictions and possessions and achievements; that I was neither centered nor grounded; that both my "earthality" and spirituality were in urgent need of long and arduous repair; that I had lost touch with my humanity—its earthiness and its saltiness, its natural and primitive side, its cosmic dimension. "You have a dark side," my ivy-shadow gently said; "you are not all light and color, as you thought; you are darkness too. You can play, as you said, but you are very selfish. Of course you can love—but you have learned now that you can also hate. You have succeeded, but remember your failures. You created much beauty, as you pointed out, but you must yet discover the destruction you left behind you. You are not perfect as you told the world you were. You are far from perfect. Even though you are an angel, always remember you have a demon too. Because I am you and you are me. But together we can transcend ourselves and reach a new divine awareness."

I was breathing freely now and the ivy was hanging loose. Faint intimations of a second spring were beginning to warm my heart, and within it, and keeping heart-beat time, a small clown was laughing silently but drumming fiercely. "Yes, my shadow," I said, "I acknowledge you and your power as part of me, and I respect the magnitude of that power. Without you I am unreal and unnatural—with no substance. But I will not forget, nor will you, what happened on the morning of the miracle when a little child revealed that the light is greater than the darkness and love is stronger than fear. We will live together but we will always be in tension." And then, as a half-serious kind of joke I told her about the Indian tribe in the Southwest who always invite Coyote, their equivalent of the shadowy trickster, to their tribal council's pow-wow and provide a place for him. Their idea, of course, is that if he is there, they can keep an eye on him, whereas if he's out of sight there is no telling what he might do![6]

The sun, who all this yearning time had grieved and hoped, was overjoyed, and joined us then. And that is how the window, the sun and the ivy—this blessed trinity of light, color and shade—began creating another plan to transform the world.

The Green Bough

Playing hide-and-seek with the world, the sun, my sister, is throwing long shadows as she slips down behind the southern ridge of Mount Diablo on the West Coast of the United States. I feel still and quiet, like someone still alive after a long and bloody battle or suddenly reprieved from a death sentence. I am filled with a profound sense of freedom and gratitude as I reflect on the prisons of my past. While unaware of the growing presence of my ivy-shadow, my addictions became more powerful and rooted. It took much effort to acknowledge and transcend these. So too with many dimensions of my life on which I came to rely and with which I began to identify—my image, my role and status, my work, my constant need for affirmation, my need for reassurance against anxiety.

During this, my second journey, my second spring, I felt the first stirrings of what could be called compassion. It was a new awareness. And "these insights do not come easily; they are gained only through severest shocks."[7] I see so clearly now the crippling self-centeredness brought about by competitiveness, ambition, compulsiveness and fragmentation. Compassion cannot share this kind of company. It can only live with gentleness and strength; with understanding and humor; with the capacity to "let go" and to "let be"; with solitude and forgiveness—and with celebration.

Compassion, that beautiful and special attribute of God's own being, will always be interwoven with wisdom. This wisdom is related to my regaining of equilibrium, my stabilization of discovery of fresh purposes and new dreams, my acceptance of limitations and death, my transcendence of suffering and evil, my acquaintance with the healing properties of paradox. Without the maturing understanding of the meaning of loving—an understanding that was birthed during the silent darkness of my long winter—the grace of compassion would have never blessed my heart. Love rarely comes easy. Even though loving is natural to us, it is still a skill. There is an apprenticeship to loving. I recalled to myself the story about the dialogue between the boy and the man who met in the city night-shelter for the poor and destitute. The man, on his way home from prison, was hoping to be reconciled with his wife who had given up on the marriage because of his selfishness. "But now I know," he said, "and it was not easy to find out. It takes a long time to discover the science of love. First I learned to love a stone and then a cloud. A long time later I knew how to love a tree and then a sparrow. Now I understand something about loving a woman." Over three hundred years ago Thomas Traherne made the same point in a more forceful and mystical way:

By love our souls are married and solder'd to the all. We must love them infinitely, but in God, and for God: and God in them: namely all His excellencies manifested in them. When we dote upon the perfections and beauties of some one creature, we do not love that too much, but other things too little. Never was anything in this world loved too much, but many things have been loved in a false way and all in too short a measure.

Suppose a river, or a drop of water, an apple or a grain of sand, an ear of corn or an herb; God knoweth infinite excellencies in it more than we; He seeth how it relateth to angels and men; how it proceedeth from the most perfect Lover to the most perfectly Beloved; how it representeth all His attributes; how it conduceth in its place, by the best of means to the best of ends: and for this cause it cannot be beloved too much. God the Author and God the End is to be beloved in it; angels and men are to be beloved in it; and it is highly to be esteemed for all their sakes. O what a treasure is every grain of sand when truly understood! Who can love anything that God made too much? His infinite goodness and wisdom and power and glory are in it. What a world would this be, were everything beloved as it ought to be.[8]

Here again in an equally forceful but perhaps less mystical way—or rather in a more earthy way—Alice Walker has Celie, in *The Color Purple,* write to Nettie about a conversation she had with her friend, Shug, about a God who was too small, who did not fit anymore and who had to be "let go of."

My first step from the old white man was trees. Then air. Then birds. Then other people. But one day when I was sitting quiet and feeling like a motherless child, which I was, it came to me: that feeling of being part of everything, not separate at all. I knew that if I cut a tree, my arm would bleed. And I laughed and cried and I run all around the house. I knew just what it was. In fact when it happen, you can't miss it. It sort of like you know what, she say, grinning and rubbing high up on my thigh.

Shug! I say.

Oh, she say, God love all them feelings. That's some of the best stuff God did. And when you know God loves 'em you enjoy 'em a lot more. You can just relax, go with everything that's going, and praise God by liking what you like.

God don't think it dirty? I ast.

Naw, she say, God made it. Listen, God love everything you love—and a mess of stuff you don't. But more than anything else, God love admiration.

You saying God vain? I ast.

Naw, she say, Not vain, just wanting to share a good thing. I think it pisses God off if you walk by the color purple in a field somewhere and don't notice it. . . . You have to git man off your eyeball, before you can see anything a tall.[9]

It is dark now. The rest of the story must wait for another day. But let me tell you one more secret. Like the sun, the ivy now was part of my life too. My heart, you will remember, had lost its power during my long hour of desolation. Early one morning when the sun, as usual, took me by surprise, it was a deep and verdant image of green that my heart was casting as it balanced on the ray of the warming sun. "Green," the ivy has often said, "is God's color. It is the color of spirit-power in motion, of all things growing, expanding and celebrating. It is the color of Spring and of creation, of all things wet and fruitful. Green is fresh and green is new; green is forever." A leaf of perfect ivy had grown across the empty space of my heart—the symbol of my creative and compassionate power. It was a thrush's song I heard:

> I am the breeze that nurtures all things green.
> I encourage blossoms to flourish with ripening fruits.
> I am the rain coming from the dew
> that causes the grasses to laugh
> with the joy of life.[10]

And my green heart was smiling too. It was smiling because we both remembered something our mother had said even as she struggled in labor to release us on to the waiting earth: "If you keep a green bough in your heart, the singing bird will come."

NOTES

1. Vernon Watkins, *Dylan Thomas: Collected Poems* (New York: New Directions, 1957) (from the poem "Fern Hill").

2. Ibid.

3. Ibid.

4. Ibid.

5. William Miller, *Make Friends with Your Shadow* (Minneapolis: Augsburg Publishing, 1982) p. 128. (Tale entitled "The King and the Corpse" from Zimmer's Collection.)

6. Ibid. pp. 135, 136.

7. Gerald O'Collins, *The Second Journey* (New York: Paulist Press, 1978) p. 56. (Quotation from "Psychological Reflections" by Carl Gustav Jung.)

8. Thomas Traherne, *Centuries* (London: Mowbray Books, 1975) p. 87.

9. Alice Walker, *The Color Purple* (New York: Washington Square Press, 1982) pp. 167, 168.

10. Gabriele Uhlein, *Meditations with Hildegard of Bingen* (Santa Fe: Bear and Co., 1982) p. 31. Quoted in Matthew Fox, *Illuminations of Hildegard of Bingen* (Santa Fe: Bear and Co., 1985) p. 31.

MAY

The Creative Heart

Something we were withholding made us weak
Until we found it was ourselves.

—ROBERT FROST

What seems different in yourself; that's the rare thing you possess. The one thing that gives each of us worth and that's just what we try to suppress. And we claim to love life.

—ANDRÉ GIDE

The Creative Heart

Behind me, thrusting proudly heavenward, were the Two Paps Mountains—the breasts of Anu, the mother-goddess of the Tuatha de Dannans who worshiped here nearly four thousand years ago. Ahead of me, in green and blue, shimmered the Atlantic Ocean, whose liquid body washed, in the distance, the East Coast of the United States of America. On this first warm day in May in the southwest of Ireland, I stood in a shallow stream and I will never forget the moment. As soon as the oozing mud pressed up between my toes, the crystal-clear water swept it away again. The sensation is totally alive in me still. It was my first day "going barefoot"—the day when, with parental permission, I shook off the leather armor that imprisoned my urgent feet which pressed themselves against the excited earth after a long winter of waiting. It is strange how vibrant still within me today is the impact through my body of my feet feeling the warm earth, the cool water, the dry timber, the cold concrete, the wet road, the soft grass and the rough gravel. . . .

One memory plucked from many. So different now. The intimacy has died. ". . . nor can foot feel, being shod," as Hopkins pointed out in "God's Grandeur." How often have I gazed at those mountains, my heart aching to be with them, to rejoice in our oneness, only to find the distance too great. So much healing and reconciling remains to be done. And just as we are wounded because we carry within us a wounded child that must be comforted before we can become creative and compassionate again, so too our deep despair and desperation can often be traced to the wounded cosmos that we also carry within us. Because we have simply lost touch . . . It is no wonder that our energies are dissipated and blocked in light of the many dichotomies within us.

Mystics over the centuries and scientists over the years have consistently reminded us of the integral part we play in the wider community of the environment. We have reflected on this in some depth in the section on The Cosmic Heart. Our comparatively recent and savage assault on our Mother-Earth will long remain one of the most baffling crimes in the history of the Universe. A very inadequate excuse might indicate that, at the time, we did not recognize her as our Mother. The horrifying story of unprovoked matricide is outlined more fully in The Dark Heart. Like the lifeless gangrenous limb that must be amputated lest it destroy the whole body, so too with us: we are on the verge of becoming amputees because the cosmic blood supply bringing health and vitality to nourish and nurture our very being has been severed—and severed by ourselves. It is a form of collective madness. It is in this profound ignorance of the interdependence of cosmos and humanity that the fundamental deficiency of the current mass schizophrenia is to be located. We have not yet comprehended, as Frank Waters points out, the psychical ecology underlying physical ecology. The Native Indians have. In ruthlessly destroying nature we, an intrinsic dimension and climax of that same nature, rupture our own inner self. We set ourselves apart not only from the earth but from the dark maternal unconscious, its psychic counterpart. Because humanity's unconscious is equated to and rooted in nature, a deeply disturbing alienation has set in. In subduing nature we have stifled the natural forces within us too—the secret and rich desires of our soul, the instincts, erotic fantasies and wild imagination of our deepest selves. This conflict, this split in the wholeness of the psyche, is, according to C. G. Jung, the tragedy of over-civilized humanity. And the battleground is the Body; and the victim is the Body; and the Body is the cosmos and my body, its offspring. Only evil wins. We must listen to the American Indians, to the friends of the Earth and to the invisible spirit of the Land itself.

A first step lies in acknowledging the presence of a strange resistance to cosmic reconciliation—a resistance born of fear. In his book *God Is Red,* the American Indian theologian Vine Deloria wrote: "White men of the West are afraid to die because they must finally recognize their oneness with the earth. In our culture there does seem to be a deep fear of our earthiness. . . ."[1] Thomas Berry and Patricia Mische in their writings, their lectures and through their respective Centers have done much to dispel these shadows and to plant the seeds of new attitudes toward the Earth. They prepare us for a long, transforming and global spiritual journey into a new age of cosmic awareness. We need a spirituality that emerges out of a reality deeper than the human, even deeper than life, a spirituality that is as deep as the earth processes itself, a spirituality that is born of the solar system and even out of the heavens beyond. The more we grow in awareness of our own sacred source, adds Mische, the more we discover that our own sacred source is the sacred source of each person and of all that is in the universe. In love everything is sacred.

A clarifying word about the structure of this section may help here. I began by suggesting that a sense of the whole and of the present is a prerequisite for the act of creating. We reflected on two of the following wounds of division that dissipate the powers within us—separations between the male and female both within ourselves and within the species, between individuals and the tribal family and between individuals/families and the wider social context of local community, between God/Love and humanity, between the rich and poor worlds, the north and south worlds, between our wounded child and ourselves and between ourselves and the universe in which we live and move and have our being. In The Eucharistic Heart we will look more closely at the beginnings of transformation and the part we can play in promoting such change of consciousness. Just now I would like to offer some creative ideas for those of us who are preparing for the holy pilgrimage into the new heaven and the new earth. Because some kind of journey is undoubtedly beginning. Intimations of an unprecedented (in recent centuries) mystical communion between humanity and the universe, a true aesthetic of the cosmos, an economy of the earth, can be perceived during still moments. Thomas Berry quotes Julia Ch'ing's phrase about humans being the "heart of the universe" and the "remarkable feeling for the absolute dimensions of the human, the total integration of reality in humankind and the total integration of humanity in reality that follows from that awareness."[2]

What is called for is a wisdom such as humanity has scarcely ever been blessed with before—a wisdom that transcends the insights, visions, analyses and strategies of yesterday's world; that is sensitively attuned to the presence of the sacred in all of Earth's processes; that can discern the urgings and allurement of the spirit in all life. Our wisdom must inform a global spirituality if our collective and sacred journey is to get under way. The healing must be happening within ourselves, between ourselves and others, between humanity and the universe. A psychic strength is called for and the courage of the cosmos itself. A new world order, a new global itinerary, a new web of undreamt-of resources and interdependent traveling companions are envisioned for this last desperate venture to save the Earth. Patricia Mische suggests the *spiral* as the appropriate image for the spiritual journey since it images inward, outward and forward movement.

These are not opposing directions, she writes, but part of a flow; a flow that develops in inner relationship to transcendental reality; in outward relationships in the human community and the whole earth community; and in forward relationships to future generations that require conscious participation in creating future history—in ongoing genesis.[3]

There is a sense in which each of us must look to ourselves before we join the larger group on the quest for survival first and then, abundant life. The first step on this threefold journey may well emerge as the longest stride of soul humanity has ever taken. Nor is it to be taken lightly. An act of creativity of such proportions, a commitment to such a sacred cause demands a passion and a patience that cannot be presupposed. Because the vision will become clouded and the story will falter; the journey will be interrupted and the spiral-image will grow faint. There will be ceaseless conflict, not pyrrhic victories; hard-won self-transcendence, not ready self-actualization; soul-sized issues, not pocket-sized problems; total commitment, not convenient contributions; the promise of suffering, not of solace.

Deeply spiritual persons experience the suffering in the world as their own suffering. Their skin is not a dividing membrane through which events flow into each other. But they do not let it overtake them and destroy their spirit, their ability to choose life. To live deeply in the spirit is to be able to see beyond the immediate evidence of brokenness. It is to seek the not yet, but possible future. To live deeply in the spirit is to find the courage to create in the midst of darkness.[4]

Creative Context

I call upon the combined vision of Berry, Mische and Swimme—a formidable and blessed trinity—to chart the course and provide the context for the creative powers to flow and unite and begin the work of transformation. Despite their keen sense of the wanton destruction being waged every moment all over the earth where precious species of non-human life are lost forever every hour of every day, and despite their infectious urgency for comrades in the race against time, they nevertheless exude a genuine and confident hope.

Berry is convinced that the long motherless period is coming to a close as we slowly come to realize the gravity of our sins against the Earth. But the roles have changed. We are now the Mother to the Earth. The child has grown to adult status. A process of renewal in the relationship has been taking place.

In this process both child and mother experience a period of alienation. Then follows a reconciliation period . . . with a new type of intimacy, a new depth of appreciation and a new mode of interdependence. Development of this new mode of earth-human communion can only take place within a profound spiritual context.[5]

Berry observes that the emergence of the new age culture will necessarily be an age dominated by the symbol of woman. The link is between the feminine and creativity. In terms of its creativity and fertility the Earth is a woman. The fate of one is the fate of the other. How similar, today, their destinies seem to be. Earth consciousness and feminine consciousness—they go together. A certain male propensity strikes out at both creators.

Our alienation from the earth, from ourselves, and from a truly creative man-woman relationship in an overly masculine mode of being, demands a reciprocal historical period in which not only a balance will be achieved but even, perhaps, a period of feminine emphasis.[6]

In an earlier reference to the feminine mystique and component of the Medieval period of Western Christendom, Berry advocates the unity, in some fashion, of Earth and Mary. "Earth needs embodiment in an historical person, so such an historical person needs an earth identity to fulfill adequately her role as divine Mother."

Another significant development for the cosmic pilgrim to be aware of is the new capacity of humanity for subjective communion with the many presences that constitute the universe. Here we are recovering the most primitive genius of humans where the world was a "spirit world" and every being

had its own divine numinous subjectivity, its self, its centre, its unique identity. Every being was a presence to every other being. . . . For this reason there is in China the universal law of compassion. When the objection was made to Wang Yangming in the 15th century that this is evident only in human relations, he replied by noting that even the frightened cry of the bird or the crushing of a plant, the shattering of a tile or the senseless breaking of a stone immediately and spontaneously causes pain in the human heart.[7]

The intimacy here seems more like identity. Tread on a daisy and trouble a star.

It is imperative for the creative and hopeful pilgrim to have a profound sense of the amazing depth of being and of the history of the ecological community. Only very recently have we been able to read the signs of the universe's origin and listen to the story of the earliest cosmic moments and, continuing since then, the many transformations of the earth. The same universe's tale is told in different ways and from a particular viewpoint by every existent being. One of the reasons for the conspiracy of protection for all living species and every living being is because of this amazing mystery of history's complete and unique presence in every entity,

A voice that is lost means knowledge and information lost to the world for all time; a story that will never again be recaptured. We must move into the future with a deep reverence for all beings and the story that each is able to tell. . . . We must understand that every living being, every community, every underwater formation rests quietly with a great realm of intelligent history folded into its being.[8]

To move us toward some kind of appreciative mind-set before we take the plunge of commitment to redeeming our Mother's failing health and beauty, Brian Swimme reminds us of our ignorance. At the moment, and in general, it is overwhelming. We do not know in either a specific or a wider sense anything about the interactions and process that will enable the future to unfold. There is one principle, however, of which we are sure: our cosmic creative unfolding and each being's individual emergence depends on the totality of evolution's previous achievement. Just as the children of the future issue directly from us who, in turn, stand on the shoulders of our ancestors, so, also, evolutionary development depends on the creative powers of everything that presently inhabits the earth system.

If we remove any species from the earth system, we are in that act forever limiting the possibilities of the future. . . . We must begin now with a profound reverence for the inherent power of self-emergence that each being possesses. . . . We are evolutionary dynamics brought into its conscious phase when we act with an awareness that these creative powers need to be evoked, defended, and nurtured with the fear and trembling that reflects our awareness of all futures that follow on our present actions.[9]

Reverent Waiting

In the meditative moments that naturally bless the heart when reflecting on issues so crucial for the quality of life now and to come, I am filled with a strong and wordless sense of silence, reverence and waiting. This attitude is the womb of creativity. Out of this quiet, still pool of emptiness flows the river of new and fresh dreams and actions. St. Thomas Aquinas wrote about "the silence of reverence." This may well be the appropriate response of men and women in the face of mystery. I associate the attitude of reverence with a heart full of wonder; but it is even more—it is laced with love. And even more than that too. There is a sense of power, like the power of a baby, and there is worship too, as when we lift a baby to our hearts. I feel reverent when a dying person smiles and when an old couple hold hands and when I listen to the stunning story of my infancy . . . twenty billion years ago . . .

The silence of reverence is about waiting. There is a stature to waiting. In a world of "instant" everything the cosmic pilgrim, if she or he is to survive and create, must develop a divine patience. Why is the sense of "waitingness" which is so powerful in great lovers, artists and almost all mothers, not just a necessary prelude to the act of creation but essentially creative in itself? When the quality and the context of the waiting is not concerned with "killing time until something happens" but is such that this is the most fruitful way to be at a given "moment," then the dynamism of creativity is at its most explosive and time itself is rendered timeless. When one "looks" at the time of waiting with the Tai Ch'i "soft eye" apprehension or reflects on it with "right-brain" appraisal, this "activity" assumes immense importance—more perhaps than the moment of "happening." The more love we feel for the world and the more meaning it has for us, then the more heightened will be the sensitivity of our waiting, and the

more intense will be the receptivity and dynamic as the various streams of consciousness meet and flow together in a new
and creative wave of divine energy. As a matter of fact it is
only IN the waiting that this can happen. Again we are aware
here of the rich folds of mystery about us. Because God also
waits. It is in waiting that God invests the world with the
possibility and power of meaning. God lies awake with humanity each night waiting for the sunrise. And while doing
so they are co-creating and conceiving in their reverent
hearts, like lovers in their waiting do, before they incarnate
their ecstasy in fine, erotic union.

   In an earlier section, The Cosmic Heart, we touched on the
phenomenon of human consciousness as the self-awareness of
the universe—the cosmic mind where the world knows itself
to be playing, grieving, celebrating, needing and so on. It is, I
believe, in this pregnant time of waiting that the world discloses to humanity its power of meaning—discloses itself in
its heights and depths, as wonder and terror, as blessing and
threat. Human receptivity here is of the same nature as God's.
The earth must be known. Urgent and necessary as the active, communal and transforming strategies of the friends of
the earth are in their structural bridge-building networking,
who would compare them to the profound moment when a
waiting lonely human being in some inner-city attic, for a
fleeting moment, UNDERSTANDS something of this fragile and beautiful world? And once understood, it is somehow
understood forever.

In and through human receptivity the world's potential for becoming wonder and terror, promise and threat, pleasure and pain,
beauty and squalor, is actualized . . . when a person receives and
recognizes the beauty of a butterfly's wing, that person is no less
enriching the totality of the world than when, by art and skill he or
she creates—if that were possible—a thing of equal beauty. [10]

It is precisely at this still point that life in the "now" is most intensely lived . . .

NOTES

1. Vine Deloria, *God Is Red* (New York: Dell Publishing Co., 1973). Quoted by Joe Holland in "The Spiritual Crisis of Modern Culture," text of seminar address sponsored by the Center of Concern (1983) p. 27.

2. Thomas Berry, "The Spirituality of the Earth," *Whole Earth Papers* (Global Education Associates, No. 16) p. 46.

3. Patricia Mische, "Toward a Global Spirituality," *Whole Earth Papers* (Global Education Associates, No. 16) p. 7.

4. Ibid. p. 13.

5. Berry, op. cit. p. 46.

6. Ibid.

7. Ibid.

8. Brian Swimme, "The New Natural Selection," *Teilhard Studies* No. 10 (1983) p. 12.

9. Ibid. p. 14.

10. Howard Vanstone, *The Stature of Waiting* (London: Darton, Longman and Todd, 1983) p. 113.

HEART'S SUMMER

A Time for Transformation

೭☙

It was difficult to make choices here in the season of transformation. There are many issues to be faced at this critical time. Issues of justice, peace and compassion, for instance, challenge for center stage. I have selected three profound dimensions of human transformation—celebrating with cosmic symbols, loving with cosmic passion and teaching with cosmic imagination—and reflected on how their truest meaning can be grasped only in terms of justice and peace, trust and compassion, power and loving play.

JUNE

The Eucharistic Heart

And I strive to discover how to signal my companions . . . to say in time a simple word, a password, like conspirators; let us unite, let us hold each other tightly, let us merge our hearts, let us create for Earth a brain and heart, let us give a human meaning to the superhuman struggle.

—Nikos Kazantzakis

Each of us is responsible for everything to everyone else.

—Fyodor Dostoevski

The Eucharistic Heart

It was a warm December in Gibraltar. The "levanter" was halfway down the Rock and the barbary apes were halfway up as I looked out over the Straits. I was preparing a talk on the Eucharist and endeavoring to propose an alternative image about its meaning. Just as the controversial gate into Spain, a few yards from where I wandered, was now open, offering new space, horizons and vistas to everybody, so too I wished to break through the closed doors of popular Eucharistic devotion. The challenge was to shift the focus from a formal, stylized liturgy that sometimes conceals rather than reveals the mysterious story of God's unconditional, universal, creative love. A history of magical attitudes toward the host "out there" on the altar had contributed to a static, individualistic and non-existential form of Eucharistic piety which had become an end in itself, divorced from life and the only "religious" time of the week.

Attitudes, however, are changing rapidly. In current theological language we speak about the Eucharist more in terms of a deeper understanding of concepts of "symbol" and "sacrament" in a community setting. We explore the various theories that attempt to describe in philosophical and theological language the transformation of bread and wine and subsequently of those who share in Communion. But still, within most of our theologies today, shades and strains of dualism are still identifiable, where the human and the divine are carefully segregated. My intentions in this "month's" reflections are to offer an approach "from below," so to speak, from the point of view of the cosmos itself—thus making a new effort to intrinsically link all the elements and all the dimensions that constitute Eucharistic celebration. In this reflection my intention is to offer to the reader a vision of the Eucharist that does not threaten orthodox doctrine but rather deepens and enriches the believer's participation at the Lord's table each week.

Celebration of a Love-Story

Sacrament, in Christian terms, is not meant to be a notion or practice imposed from without, but rather to be regarded in light of a world already filled and permeated with Love's essence—a world that tends toward the celebration in symbol and word of its own amazing story, beauty and hopes. The symbolic power of the sacramental action is to remember, affirm, celebrate and intensify the love and meaning at the heart of all creation; to remind ourselves, as the Incarnation did, that dualism is not from God, and that in truth, in historical reality, Love has always been incarnate.

Everything which God created millions of years ago and everything which will be created by God after millions of years . . . God is creating all that in the innermost and deepest realms of the soul. God's being is my being and God's primordial being is my primordial being. Wherever I am, there is God.[1]

Everyone is graced with the capacity for this vision. For each one, as for Francis of Assisi, the sun and moon, fire and water, the four directions and all the elements, animals and humans—all creatures—are windows on God, or, more accurately, faces of God. Even the smallest particle of creation is a theophany, a sacrament, a revelation of God.

Apprehend God in all things, urges Meister Eckhart, for God is in all things. Every single creature is full of God and is a book about

God. Every creature is a word of God. If I spent enough time with the tiniest creature—even a caterpillar—I would never have to prepare a sermon. So full of God is every creature.[2]

We therefore need new eyes to read the wind, sand and stars, people's hands, hearts and faces, beneath the first level of appearance. It is the vision of the heart we search for here. "It is only with the heart that one sees clearly," explains the Little Prince; "what is essential is invisible to the eye." There are surprises and special gifts to help us all make this transition— moments which stand out from all the others, gracious moments when the paradigm shifts and a single leaf becomes every tree, each holy stream is the underground river of Love, a rock speaks prophecies and a smile transforms a winterheart. We say that such small epiphanies are sacramental because in them we glimpse through windows of wonder something of the joy of God incarnate in everything.

The famous local cloud was lifting now over the Rock and the sun picked out the Mediterranean colors of a trim sailingboat as, at one with the skillful hands that urged and guided it, it turned neatly and moved gracefully and seemingly miraculously to the east into the very wind that just now had filled its westward-bound sails. And my heart sang. Because I too was changing course, transcending all I knew. I returned to my thoughts. The Eucharist, I began to see, is such a sacramental moment, ritualized into certain times and places. The actual emotional vision, the inspirational moment, rarely coincides with the actual formal ceremony but nevertheless the Eucharist becomes more exciting and alluring when participated in as a liturgical celebration of a life already sacramental in its own right by virtue of creation—the first incarnation.

The Eucharist then is of a piece with the rest of reality and life; it is the institutionalized expression in symbol of a story of love as felt in human hearts. These hearts are, in turn, the self-expression in human consciousness of the evolving love-story of the universe. And before that again, the whole cosmos, of which the universe is a part, is the self-expression, in time and space, of the first divine love in the heart of God. The bread and the wine, therefore, around which we would soon gather, have a long history. The seeds, in fact, were planted a long time ago, in bright darkness, before time began.

A butterfly, almost subliminally, fluttered by without a greeting as if fearful of distracting me. I think she sensed that I was catching up on the wisdom already safely entrusted to her tiny heart. She knew too how important it was that we humans should get it right. So I began again to think carefully.

Creation had waited for billions of years to achieve self-consciousness. Once this breakthrough was accomplished, the cosmos then needed to celebrate its incredible life-story with its mysterious beginning, its hazardous evolution, its split-second timing and its relentless success. For with the advent of humanity—its new, first and unique heart and mind—this became possible. And the Eucharist is one of its rich expressions. And this expression has to be symbolic—there is no other way that such a cosmic love-story could be encapsulated in time and space. "The earth, like an apple, is placed on the table." In the sacramental mode, with bread and wine, the world is acknowledging its very being as flowing from the womb of God at the beginning of time and in each passing moment. Through the human voices, gestures and sacramental action of its offspring, the universe is in worship before its Creator, offering itself to its incomprehensible lover-God in the ecstasy of its joys and the bitterness of its sorrows.

There is, of course, more to the Eucharist than the long-awaited celebration of exulting joy, praise and thanksgiving as the patient soul of the Earth finally evolved into a richer mode of life in its humanity. What I mean is that humanity itself, in its breakthrough into intelligence and human love, has, especially in its famous visionaries, prophets and messiahs, been able to reflect back to its cosmic ancestry, very sketchy but unbelievably exciting revelations about its origins, history of evolution and maybe even its destiny. The Eucharist brings to self-consciousness, identifies and names for the universe some of the deepest dimensions of its miraculous growth. It achieves this because, once upon a time, a human being, a Man, one of those at the forefront of the evolutionary journey, enlightened by Love herself, recapitulated in his life, death and resurrection what is already going on in the birth from nothingness of the cosmos, and in the dying and living that is the constant in its growth. There is, therefore, a central and stunning truth revealed and celebrated in the eucharistic drama. Because of the history of this Man, millions of people believe that the ubiquitous death built into the innermost heart of the cosmos and of every creature of life is essential to the love that powers the universe relentlessly onward to the glorious realization of our full dignity and majesty.

The play and struggle between the dying and rising in the loving heart of the living cosmos, together with the eventual outcome of delight of that sometimes bloody conflict, is revealed, clarified, named, owned, and celebrated by the universe at every true Eucharistic gathering, "with a directness and an intensity like that of the Incarnation itself."[3] Thus in a ritual in time and space, involving bread and wine and words, in one privileged and symbolic moment, the eternal significance of the mighty cosmos is encapsulated.

The Eucharistic Conspiracy

In the dynamic presence of the bread and wine on the table we have symbolized just about everything that can be predicated of humanity, the Earth and everything on and in it, the universe and the cosmos itself—the past, present and future of all creation. These rich and simple elements gather up the intense agony and ecstasy of the world, its darkness and light, its failures and mistakes, its strivings and hopes, its indomitable creativity.

I will place on my paten, O God, the harvest to be won by this renewal of labour. Into my chalice I shall pour all the sap which is to be pressed out this day from the earth's fruits. One by one Lord I see and I love all those whom you have given me to sustain and charm my life. One by one also I number all those who make up that other beloved family which has gradually surrounded me, its unity fashioned out of the most disparate elements, with affinities of the heart, of scientific research and of thought. And again, one by one, I call before me the whole vast anonymous army of living humanity. . . . All the things in the world to which this day will bring increase; all those that will diminish; all those too that will die. . . . This is the material of my sacrifice . . . the offering you really want, the offering you mysteriously need every day to appease your hunger, to slake your thirst is nothing less than the growth of the world borne ever onwards in the stream of universal becoming.[4]

   And then the eternal words of disclosure are spoken: "This is my Body." They sound around this Earth and they echo around the stars. They were whispered by our loving Mother when the terrible beauty of the fiery atoms shattered the infinite darkness of space with unimaginable flame, heat and light. And God has waited for her creation to unfold in the power of her own love, and, in that unfolding, the cosmos became self-reflecting in the consciousness of humanity. And it is this human awareness, that repeats again the words first heard in its infancy many years before, when God spoke her creative words into the void, "This is my Body." It is God-become-atom, become-galaxies, become-stars, become-universes, become-Earth, become-human that speaks these words to her own body in a human voice, "This is my Body." It is a remembering, a reminding and a confirming that the divine and the human, the sacred and the secular, the holy and the profane are all God's one body by virtue of creation, first in Time but revealed to us later in the Incarnation.

The Cosmic Dance of Bread and Wine

I am aware here of being drawn to reconnect the Eucharistic ritual with a deeper pagan, pre-Christian, pre-Hebrew vision and practice. The world, for those who lived in an earlier tribal age, was filled with spirits and psychic power-symbols. Their lives were guided toward communion with each other and with the environment. The archetypal sense of a total cosmic presence that went beyond the surface reality of the surrounding natural world sustained the tribes in their human, social and artistic development. This spiritual consciousness emerged into mental symbols and finally into visible expression.

All that humankind has done since then has taken this same course. The gods have been changed, the visible expression has been altered, but the ultimate source of power still remains hidden in the dynamics of the earth and in the obscure archetypal determinations of the unconscious human depths.[5]

The Christian tradition of Eucharistic celebration has not always acknowledged its roots in such a blessed land. This celebration therefore may be regarded as another way of opening ourselves to the current of this same universal, eternal dynamic; of celebrating its present reality and of reminding us of our responsibility for the vital role (now that we have come of age) that we play in the cosmic unfolding into the future. The bread and wine have, indeed, a long and proud story to tell. And where else can the story be told—or rather danced—as appropriately as on the Eucharistic dance-table where the primal rhythm has never been lost? The cosmic drum is beating and with a flash of her eye and a hitch of her skirts Gaia⁶ leaps to the table. And the dance begins . . .

The swaying troupes, dancing by heart and without rehearsal, form a kaleidoscopic pattern of natural and common movement. Love, we know, is dancing at the heart of creation and in every created heart. Matter itself is a whirling mass of rhythmic patterns and synchronized movement. The human words and gestures are a graceful and reverent kind of ballet that blend with and integrate the various dimensions of the cosmic choreography. In Love, cosmic, human and divine, celebrated as one, we live and dance and have our being.

Sometimes the drum-beat is slow and the mood is created by memories. The story is told about the bread and wine, the fruit of the earth and the work of human hands, and about their infancy in the childhood of the universe billions of years ago, and about their conception in the womb of the Creator-lover, as she danced the first dance. The bread and wine, our proud ancestors on the family tree of life, remind us of their new and unique responsibility as Eucharistic symbols of love, justice and peace for ever.

At other times the dance is to a lament. The mood is anxious as the tale unfolds. The lament is for the wanton damage inflicted upon all our relations within the cosmos—a crime that springs from human ignorance, carelessness and greed. Bread—the harvest of labor, the product of toil and sweat. And wine—the strained juice of pain, the sap of suffering. The Love that begot the world—and that lives within it now, carrying these scars forever—is asked to forgive us for this truly mortal sin. But the lamentations are not despairing—their power will transform the reality of evil.

More often than not, the dance is a playful time—the kind of play that is adventurous and free. The bread and wine here symbolize the playfulness of creating and the creativity of play. The elements themselves have played in the growing and harvesting of the wondrous wheat and grain. Air, fire, earth and water change their formations and patterns appropriately and flawlessly with the circling seasons and the changing directions, so that, from east to west, a perfect sacrifice of praise may reverberate around the planets. The laugh of the cosmos can be heard as it trusts the love that has already become conscious in humanity and subsequently realized its divinity in a unique and sacramental way in One (at least) of those who made the awesome step into human consciousness—God's special work of art.

Above all the dance is a celebration by the cosmos of its own exquisite beauty, relentless success and ultimate destiny. In light of the new spiritual power released by the flowering cosmic energy in the breakthrough of One human person into Love herself, the surprised cosmos celebrates its divinity. It was revealed in this Special One, who himself was the human consciousness of the Love-inspired and Love-sustained universe—a divine Love that was the origin and destiny of all existence. The cosmic celebration, therefore, honors the communion and unity both at its heart already and for which it forever yearns. Human interlinking and interdependence is now a reality bringing about the birth of a planetary mind and soul.

Today a new light has dawned upon the world
Love has become one with humanity
and humanity has become one again with Love.

The eternal Word has taken upon himself
our earthy condition
giving our human nature divine value.
So enchanting is this communion between Love
and humanity
that in Christ the world bestows to itself
the gift of
Love's own life.
—Christmas Preface III: The Roman Missal (my translation)

Becoming the Vision

In Eucharistic celebration it is WE who are changed and re-aligned with our true nature. Taking part in Communion "does nothing other than transform us into that which we consume."[7] Jean Luis Segundo suggests that we should not just be "gospel consumers" but "gospel creators." Perhaps Christians should make continual efforts to authenticate their sacramental life by being not only "Eucharist consumers" but of necessity "Eucharist creators" too, committed to establishing a new world order in which the universe itself is seen as the Body of God in which the basic needs of all humanity are provided for and the resources of the world justly shared. The fact that the Eucharist is today celebrated in a world where over one thousand million people are regularly hungry asks a profound question of all Eucharist consumers. Sean McDonagh devotes his book to this issue.

Hunger, malnutrition, lack of opportunities to grow and harvest food, the erosion of the genetic base of our staple foods, the control of seeds by a few giant companies and the continual degradations of fertile croplands are all interrelated. One cannot celebrate the Eucharist today without being challenged to do something about this appalling reality.[8]

When we eat the bread and drink the wine we are identifying in the most complete way with the cosmos and with the love that created and continues to create it. We symbolically transform the cosmos into our very lives just as the cosmos will one day transform us into its body. Full participation in the Eucharistic celebration should not be entered into lightly. We may not be able to afford the cost of discipleship. Our desire for justice and peace among the family of humanity and in the non-human kingdom may not be, as yet, passionate enough. The original sin of humanity lies in the lack of hunger for community. "The only real fall of humanity is its non-eucharistic life in a non-eucharistic world."[9]

In light of new cosmological insights I am here involved in revisioning theological language and concepts. If I am on the right track, a startlingly fresh and simple image of truth emerges. In the bread and wine of the Eucharistic encounter, in the intimate inter-identification of my personal love-filled body with the wider love-filled body of the cosmos and so of God, the three loves (or rather the same Love with different faces) earnestly converse around the fireside of my heart. They swap stories as they revisit the albums of yesterday, affirm the present and discuss the journey of destiny with hope and courage. At times such as this, when Love comes a-visiting, the house of my heart is filled with amazement at the beauty of its guest; it is filled with gratitude at her wild extravagance; it is filled with reverence as it savors the presence of this gracious lady. It is a house of blessings; but blessings must travel. And so, in rapture, the chimneys ring with the music of praise. And these tunes of glory waltz their way of wonder onto the cosmic dance-floors of the very heavens themselves . . .

Let me review this image again. The creative Love of the universe that has relentlessly inspired the evolutionary journey of its own Body, guiding it through the crucial breakthroughs in its quest for human love, negotiating the deadly temptations toward extremes—either those of random and aimless selection or premature closure—urging it along the cosmic milestones of destiny, this tremendous Lover is really and truly present in the fruit of her Body, this bread and wine. She is sacramentally alive and playing, running wild across the countryside of my heart. That this mysterious and lovely story is true we know because that same Love has now revealed it to be so. She has revealed it in One of her favorite children, graced through his human consciousness in an extraordinary manner with the very vision of Love herself. Quite recent in the evolutionary calendar, this cosmic moment of disclosure exploded with the same split-second and perfect timing that marked all previous breakthroughs of universal import. Among many stunning insights into the love and meaning at the heart of creation, this revealing vision perceives the Eucharistic dynamic (and a rich variety of such ritualistic celebrations) as intrinsic to, expressing, purifying and intensifying the conspiracy of trust and the networking of love, while, like a divine spring, the Holy Spirit rides her dream into tomorrow, singing the silence, filling the empty and birthing the not-yet.

This loving Eucharistic dialogue is therefore of cosmic significance always and, by definition, cannot be particularized or trivialized into partisanship, nationalism or anything that smacks of prejudice or subtle manipulation. These days, viewed from a universal perspective however, Eucharistic celebration reveals a shocking situation. Because I see, first thing each Sabbath morning, as we sit with our divine visitor at the sacramental table of broken bread and poured-out wine, the surprised, even astonished expression of hurt and pain in those lovely eyes, as the guest of our souls reveals to us in silence her freshly scarred and disfigured body. This was not the work of an enemy. Nor was the mutilation maliciously intended. It was, incredibly, the work of thoughtless, greedy children, now grown stronger than their mother. For many a long winter this heavy shadow will continue to fall across each truly Eucharistic table. It will take many a spring of healing before the first and final bright Eucharist at the moment of noon or in the rich and fertile darkness of the midnight hour will signal and establish the community of compassion, justice and peace in a cosmos of love. There will be seasons of painstaking plowing, trusting seeding, erotic greening and festive harvesting before the prodigal children would "come to their senses" and recognize, love and honor—finally—the body of their Mother of which this piece of broken bread is the Blessed Sacrament.

Healing a Broken Body

The experience of sharing and consuming Love's Body, the Blessed Sacrament of the Universe, the Cosmic Bread of Incarnate Divinity, the Sacred Wine of a Growing Humanity, the Holy Communion of all forms of Life, brings, as well as deep joy, forebodings, where the future appears as a yawning chasm into which a mutilated and drained earth must fall. Let us look briefly at some reasons for such deep concern.

Thomas Berry writes about the failing of our present energy sources as pollution darkens the skies and poisons the seas, as tensions between nations and within nations intensify, as military methods grow more destructive, as the multitudes of humankind double in numbers and people swarm toward the urban centers of crime and violence. The labor-saving and leisure-filling dimensions of the technological and industrial breakthroughs were creative, appropriate and very welcome. But in a turbulent age of change where political power and social sin are liable to run wild, the earth was exploited in irrevocable ways. Savage assaults were made upon the environment and people became destructive beyond imagination. The discoveries that initially brought enrichment and satisfaction to human hearts later "went to the heads" of power-oriented men and emerged as manipulation and exploitation of all life-levels. The experience of sacred communion with the earth went underground, so to speak, waiting, in the darkness, to be rediscovered and nurtured into vibrant life. Human power over life and death has become frighteningly efficient.

For the first time they (humans) can intervene directly in the genetic process. For the first time they can destroy the ozone layer that encircles the earth and let the cosmic radiation bring about distortions in the life process. For the first time they can destroy the complex patterns of life in the seas and make our rivers uninhabitable by any form of life. Some areas of river pollution are so bad now that not even bacteria can live in them.[10]

In its wantonness human power reaches destructively everywhere over the very topography of the planet from the emptying of the earth of its precious topsoil to the filling of space with flying junk.

Berry numbers this change in the relation of human activity to the earth process among the major shifts of evolution such as the transition from non-life to life or from life to consciousness. I have no doubt that when the hoped-for awakening consciousness and the redeeming vision of humanity assume the fullness of spiritual power, the resultant transformation of the universe will rank with the morning of creation itself. What is at stake is a matter of

. . . the interior richness within our own personalities, of shared understanding and sympathy in our homes and in our families. Beyond this is our extended security and inter-communion with others in an embrace of mind and heart that reaches out to the local community, to the nation, to the larger world of humanity, to an affectionate concern for all living and non-living beings of earth, and on out to the most distant stars in the heavens. . . .[11]

As we take, break, share, eat and drink the cosmic bread and wine and turn to embrace the stranger at the "kiss of peace" how aware are we of the kind of dying we may be called upon to make!

Let us plant dates, even though those who plant them will never eat them. . . . We must live by the love of what we will never see. This is the secret discipline. It is a refusal to let the creative act be dissolved away in immediate sense experience, and a stubborn commitment to the future of our grandchildren. Such disciplined love is what has given prophets, revolutionaries and saints the courage to die for the future they envisaged. They make their own bodies the seed of their highest hope.[12]

In one sense we are at the beginning now. There is a mission of cosmic proportions to be accomplished—a world to win and a universe to save and a Body to be healed. To live the Ritual. To be the Myth. To see the world as God sees it; to love it into health as God does. "The eye with which I see God is the same eye with which God sees me."[13] "How do we acquire a new vision? How do we inspire the unconscious heart of humanity? Who will re-create the human species as an intrinsic development of cosmic evolution, as a child of the universe? Who will set the context for re-inhabiting the earth?"[14]

A massive re-education of the heart is called for. Luckily we have the teachers. There is also, it seems to me, a readiness for change, a potential for transformation. There is a growing sensitivity to new strategies of concern, a kind of genetic awareness of the need for imminent action. There are pockets of conspirators all over the world; and when these small streams of consciousnesses seem to make but little headway into the dry mainland, we must believe that at another invisible level, the waves of transformation are already sweeping through: "For while the tired waves vainly breaking/Seem here no painful inch to gain/Far back, through creeks and inlets making/Comes silent, flooding in, the main."

By this time the shadows had gathered quietly all around me and the apes were sleeping on the lap of the eternal Rock. I tiptoed home.

NOTES

1. Matthew Fox, *Meditations with Meister Eckhart* (Santa Fe: Bear and Co., 1983) pp. 20 and 25.

2. Ibid. p. 14.

3. John McQuarrie, *Principles of Christian Theology* (London: SCM Press, 1966) p. 398.

4. Teilhard de Chardin, *Hymn of the Universe,* (New York: Harper and Row, 1961) pp. 19–20.

5. Thomas Berry, "The Ecological Age," *Whole Earth Papers* No. 12 (Global Education Associates, 1979) p. 7.

6. Ancient Greek name for the Earth. Recently proposed by the novelist William Golding as the name for the personification of the hypothesis of science which postulates that the climate and the composition of the Earth remain always at the most appropriate levels for whatever life inhabits it.

7. Vatican Council II, *The Dogmatic Constitution on the Church,* par. 26.

8. Sean McDonagh, *To Care for the Earth* (Santa Fe: Bear and Co., 1987) p. 171.

9. Alexander Shmemann, *The World as Sacrament* (London: Darton, Longman and Todd, 1974) p. 19.

10. Berry, p. 8.

11. Ibid. p. 5.

12. Rubern Alves, *Tomorrow's Child* (New York: Harper and Row, 1972). Quoted in Patricia Mische, "Toward a Global Spirituality," *Whole Earth Papers* No. 16, p. 11.

13. Fox, p. 21.

14. I have in mind here the kind of inspiration that is generated at the Institute for Culture and Creation-Centred Spirituality in Oakland, California, by its Director, its staff and visiting speakers. Thomas Berry, for example, has clarified for many the basic structure of the Fourth (Ecological) Age. In talks and writings he has introduced his audiences to his "Twelve Principles for Understanding the Universe and the Role of the Human in the Universe Process." For further essential reading in this area, check the bibliography under Mische, Swimme, Fox and McDonagh.

JULY

The Erotic Heart

God speaks . . .
When your easter comes
   I shall be around you,
   I shall be through and through you
     And I shall steal your body
     And give you to your love
     —MECHTILD OF MAGDEBURG

   God possesses the heavens
   but he covets the earth
   . . . oh, he covets the earth
       —W. B. YEATS

The Erotic Heart

The fabric of this section is woven from selected strands of mysticism and eroticism. It also has threads of the elemental attraction that we experience toward the fusion of the finite and the infinite—the cosmic call of evolving love that arises from within and from without. It has something to do with what I hesitantly designate as sexual self-transcendence where nothing is lost and everything is gained. This whole dimension of humanity does not lend itself easily to definition or description even. It has to do with the "pattern that connects," as Gregory Bateson puts it, and the insight into the phenomenon comes only in glimpses.

The quantum change in the psyche's identity takes place as one realizes that the self, like light, is simultaneously a particle and a wave. . . . In the unitive glimpse, we see the self-spirit as belonging both within the collection of individuals that make up the multiverse and within the network of life that makes up the universe.[1]

What happens can be called a shift in perception or identity, with less interest in answers and a whole new agenda of questions—questions about the search into the place and space and strategy for being more fully present to the Beauty of which we are already a part.

Divine Intimacy

Many will regard this world-view with either fear, contempt or ridicule. Some will humorously tolerate it as the romantic fantasy of a naive mind. There is an ever-increasing number, however, who are becoming more committed to an apprehension of all creation as the gradual manifestation of the glory of Love incarnate, the harmony of God coming into earshot, the praise-filled becoming of Being itself. The story is one of loving creation, pro-creation and co-creation. It is therefore about relationship. All kinds of inter-relating, inter-connecting, inter-depending and intercoursing. And every new birth is another sign of new hope. The mystics can "see" that whatever is new anywhere is new everywhere. For them, all boundaries have collapsed. There is only inter-penetration. Even where God is concerned. "Between God and humanity," writes Julian of Norwich, "there is no between." The queendom of grace is everywhere. So many spend their lives in search of the "sacred place." The pilgrimage may be to this temple, to that shrine, to the "holy person" who knows the way. But every hour is a holy hour and every place a sanctuary. We search for a place that has never been really lost because we are standing on it. That is why the pilgrim's peak experience destroys the holy mountain! " 'When we get there,' as Gertrude Stein said, 'there is no there there.' The moment the self arrives at the vision of the unity of the cosmos, the eye (the I) that sees is dissolved into what is seen."[2] The roots of such a creation-centered cosmology and theology go back a very long way in the spiritual history of our world. In the thirteenth century Meister Eckhart reminded us that "heaven still invades the earth, energizes it and makes it sacred. . . . God is at home: it is we who have gone out for a walk."[3]

Indeed, the love-story began a long time before that. Impatient with male imagery of a masculine God, some contemporary theologians are re-emphasizing more feminine models of God in an effort to breathe new life into the relationship between the Creator and ourselves—a relationship grown dry from inadequate images and metaphors. They strive toward a grounding and an earthing in concepts and language, that is often absent in current considerations of Christian spirituality. They insist on taking the fact of Incarnation at its face value. In defense of divine-human passion, Phyllis Trible refers to the Hebrew scriptures. "Thus I hear the Song of Songs. It speaks from lover to lover with whispers of intimacy, shouts of ecstasy and silences of consummation. At the same time, its unnamed voices reach out to include the world in its symphony of eroticism."[4] A current model of the world as God's body is providing welcome space for a new dynamic. It suggests that God loves bodies; in loving the world God loves a body. Wherever in the universe, for instance, there is new life, ecstasy and fulfillment, God experiences these pleasures and rejoices with each creature in its joy. God of course, is also involved profoundly, palpably and personally in the dark and sinister reality of a suffering world.

This pantheistic-type model of the world as God's body offends many. So do some others, such as God as Mother or God as Friend. People are uncomfortable with the implied intimacy. All overtones of passion or desire in God's love for creatures is somehow threatening. This is especially true in the image of God as lover. Accustomed as we are to calling God "Love" we find it unacceptable to regard her as a lover. This anxiety is gradually being transcended. Medieval mysticism has so much to offer here. Bernard of Clairvaux describes the Incarnation as a divine-human kiss—God's mouth kisses the mouth of humanity. "Happy kiss . . . in which God is united with his creatures. . . ."[5] Another example of the lover-model occurs in the writings of Mechtild of Magdeburg, a thirteenth century mystic. "I am in you and you are in me. We could not be any closer. We two are fused into one, poured into a single mould. Thus, unwearied, we shall remain forever."[6] There is more than "naive sexuality"[7] in these passionate outpourings of the same mystic:

My soul is in highest bliss,
for she has seen
and thrown her arms around
her Loved One all at one.
Poor thing,
she is distressed by him;
he so draws and delights her
she cannot withhold herself
and he brings her into himself.[8]

Meister Eckhart has no inhibitions, either, about using rich, erotic language to model God's relationship with his creatures. "It is a joy to God to have poured out the divine nature and being completely into us who are divine images. The seed of God is in us."[9] Yet another thirteenth-century mystic, Gertrude of Helfta, images God as ". . . the delicate taste of intimate sweetness, most delicate caresser . . . most ardent lover. . . ."[10] Something of the divine desire for the beloved is evident in this quaint entry in the autobiographical writings of W. B. Yeats. The reference is to his great contemporary Irish writer, George Russell (A.E.). ". . . Russell had just come in from a long walk on the Two Rock Mountain, very full of his conversation with an old religious beggar who kept repeating 'God possesses the heavens but He covets the earth—He covets the earth.' "[11]

Sally McFague's new book makes for delightful reading. She writes theology for an ecological, nuclear age that gives pride of place to feminist reflection. She pays much attention to the notion of "value." The crux of being in love is "value." It is finding someone else valuable and being found valuable. Being found valuable, she points out, is the most complete affirmation possible. It says I love you just because you are you; I delight in your presence, you are precious beyond all saying to me. Her reflections here are by way of preparing us for a later theological statement about the nature of redemption which she wishes to present as the action of a lover, not a restorer. She understands salvation as the making whole or uniting with what is attractive and valuable, rather than as the rescuing of what is sinful and worthless.

McFague expresses in warm exciting language some of the truths about God's love for the world already acknowledged by earlier theologians but in a less poetic and more clinical language. She quotes one of her students:

There is passion in the universe; the young stars, the whirling galaxies—the living, pulsing earth thrives in the passionate embrace of life itself. Our love for one another is the language of our passionate God. . . . It is desire that spins us round, desire that sends the blood through our veins, desire that draws us into each other's arms and onward in the lifelong search for God's face. And in the love of one another we see that face—in the touch of each other's hands we feel God's presence.[12]

God as lover, she writes, is the one who loves the world not with the fingertips but totally and passionately, "taking pleasure in its variety and richness, finding it attractive and valuable, delighting in its fulfillment."[13]

Cosmic Intimacy

As with God and God's creation, so too with humanity and the universe. It is "we," not "I." Within my permeable skin live a billion cells organized into elaborate communes called heart, liver, bone and brain.

When the moon is full and the sea swells, my sleep is restless because some surge that links the stars and the atoms washes through my body like the tide. And plants and cats and other living things tune to the vibrations I send and bloom and purr, or shrink from my hostile intent. When I am tuned to the rhythms of my inspiration and expiration I remember that I am a coming together of a community of atoms. I am a little world, a microcosm. Everything that is happening anywhere in the world is happening in me. The moon rises in my blood; lilacs bloom in my nostrils; suns are born and burst in the atoms that are my substance. I am one body with the world.[14]

The cynics would regard such an attitude of consecration as childish foolishness in a world that is being ravaged and desecrated. Depending on how one interprets those words they might be right. There is something of the imaginative gracefulness and wonder-filled magic of childhood in such a conviction. There is something vulnerable and powerful about adults with a kind of primal trust that they are at the center of a cosmic, intricate dance-pattern where nothing happens by chance. But with time, the conviction grows. "It seems as if the moment that I decide to trust the world to provide the daily meaning and direction I need to live in harmony, ordinary events turn into omens that instruct me."[15] Even though in the minority, there are physicists, theologians and philosophers with a mystical turn of mind, who are comfortable with such a world-view. The list grows daily and it is so exciting to listen to their different ways of presenting the same vision. This vision is the central theme, for instance, of the priest-scientist Teilhard de Chardin.

Through every cleft, the world we perceive floods us with riches—food for the body, nourishment for the eyes, the harmony of sounds and fullness of the heart, unknown phenomena and new truths—all these treasures, all these stimuli, all these calls coming to us from the four corners of the world, cross our consciousness at every moment. What is their role within us? They will merge into the most intimate life of our soul, and either develop it or poison it.[16]

The writer and psychologist Sam Keen has an equally poetic style in his description of the same communal and compassionate consciousness:

The more I act as if I were the nexus of some loving conspiracy, the
more messages I receive, the more synchronicities happen, the more
I come together with my cosmic environment and lose my sense of
being an alienated atom in a billiard-ball universe, the more porous I
become to the waves-vibrations-intrusions-invitations of other people, animals, vegetables and minerals that co-habit this planet.[17]

Making (Mystical) Love

This extraordinary allurement is in our hearts and forever will
be. Because, out of context, we are lonely fragments. We are
spiritually disconnected, like a swallow without air, a salmon
without water, a mole without earth, a moth without fire.
We yearn for a home we never really left, a womb that is
always greater than its fruits. Cosmic isolation is more painful than solitary confinement. This kind of alienation can be
healed only when we discover a transcending bonding. And
there is no end to the list of strategies (many are counterfeit)
that we employ to assuage the relentless demand of the
spiritually-lonely heart. Mystics, like prophets and gold, can
be true or false, and all have their moments on the stage of
mystical drama—in a contemporary mystery-play of destiny.
One way or another we need to be re-MINDed to re-
MEMBER who we truly are—that our breath is a part of
BREATH, our love is a part of LOVE and our life is a part of
LIFE. To achieve this consciousness, to deepen its reality and
to celebrate both, we chant and sing, we meditate and worship, we dance and ritualize. And sometimes we come up
with new and exciting ceremonies and creations of our own

imagination. The finely-honed soul of the monk, Thomas Merton, longed for multiple unity. It was as though his body-spirit wished to become a playground for adventurous encounters, a meeting-point for making new connections, a prism that gathers, transforms and scatters so many rays of light, a focus for intercourse at various levels of Being.

One might say, he writes, I had decided to marry the silence of the forest. The sweet dark warmth of the whole world will have to be my wife. Out of the heart of that dark warmth comes the secret that is heard only in silence, but it is the root of all the secrets that are whispered by all the lovers in their beds all over the world. So perhaps I have an obligation to preserve the stillness, the silence, the poverty, the virginal point of pure nothingness which is at the center point of all other loves. I attempt to cultivate this plant without comment in the middle of the night and water it with psalms and prophecies in silence. It becomes the most rare of all the trees in the garden, at once the primordial paradise tree, the axis mundi, the cosmic axle, and the Cross.[18]

Merton, like Sam Keen and Norman O. Brown after him, is trying to liberate Eros from its genital moorings and envision a life in which a person would be connected to the entire environment with an intensity that was once reserved for the genital connection. "The point is not that genital sexuality is abandoned, but that it ceases to be the dominant form of intercourse. To be animated by a vision of the unity of all things is to see that intercourse is the fundamental fact of the universe; it is not an act that must be accomplished."[19] The question here concerns the restoration of a lost balance. We are all children of the same Mother and our love will always and only be true when it honors that tradition. I would like to reflect further on this issue of balance in the context of loving human beings making love.

. . . we cohabit either lovingly or carelessly. And our erotic impulses are fully satisfied only when we are within an environment in which we are continually stimulated to care and to enjoy. Eros is fully engaged only when we make the cosmic connection. Sexual love is both most passionate and most ordered when it assumes its rightful position within a nexus of erotic relationships that make up the natural world. Earthy love begins when we acknowledge our participation in an ecological bonding that joins all the species of life in a single commonwealth.[20]

It may appear quaint or pretentious to hold that the power and energy of the act of human intercourse can be traced back to the original fire before time began. It happens, however, to be true.

I am saying that if we are going to think about (human) love in its cosmic dimension, we must start with the universe as a whole. We must begin with the attraction that permeates the entire macrostructure. I'm speaking precisely of the basic binding energy found everywhere in reality. I'm speaking of the primary allurement. . . .[21]

Looked at in another way and in light of the point so often made in this book—that humanity is the special, long-awaited love-child of the cosmos—it seems as though one of the moments that the universe sorely needed in the life of its emerging consciousness was the holy moment of the unique and supreme act of love between two human beings thus allowing the cosmos itself to express the love in its heart. Itself, as we have seen, no stranger to allurement, enchantment, coupling and expanding, the cosmos felt incomplete until the mystery of co-creation continued to unfold in its humanity, i.e. us. We provide the cosmos with the ability to make love in a new and special way.

This whole concept is rather difficult to pin down. There is a sense in which every second carries the world on its back. It is on this moment, this eternal "now," this sacrament of the present instant, that all history hangs. The infinite and the finite meet again and again, at every split-second. Eternity, in a manner of speaking, needs the point of time in which to express its incarnate cosmic thrust, telescoped into limitation for explosive power. When this moment is the vessel of totally expressed human love, a rainbow stretches over the valley of the lovers with a benediction of color. Because each couple making love are powered in their passion, whether they know it or not, by nothing less than cosmic energy. There is a sense in which every union that ever happened, from and including the first milli-second of creation, is caught up, affirmed and celebrated by each act of love between loving humans. This moment in time is the sacrament of the timeless love of our Creator-Mother, and of the history of the universe. Cut off from its cosmic roots and power our love-making will be less than true. Because the feeling point of sexual pleasure, if it is true to love, carries a cosmic intensity in its ecstasy. It is no more and no less than the divine and creative penetration of the gods in their intercourse with creation. It is a holy moment because it is timeless and eternal. After aeons of waiting, all things unite in that explosion of love. When lovers lie down, the galaxies shiver in anticipation. When they get up, God claps her hands in pure joy.

Cosmic Marriage

Let me end this section with an invitation—to a cosmic wedding. Kim is Oriental, yellow, and female; Daniel is European, white, male. But we both knew our hearts to be the human expression of the eternal love of the cosmos-made-flesh, and we both knew these same hearts to be the playground of the universe, where the humor of creation would become conscious of itself in our lifting hearts, and the surprise in evolution would become self-aware in their faster beating. We knew ourselves to be called to something very special by our Mother Earth; there was a role we had to play, a bond we had to secure, a covenant to establish. Something that had never been done before and, once appropriately completed, would never have to be repeated. We would prepare ourselves with sweat, fasting and prayer.

The Grand Canyon, the holy album of the centuries, the playground of the ages would be the sacred setting for the Cosmic Wedding. As we sat on a hill overlooking San Francisco Bay one red evening in early Spring, we talked about the earth, the universe and the cosmos that we loved and felt loved by. It was then that we decided to create a ritual of love and compassion, of forgiveness and reconciliation, of healing and of wholeness. It would be a ritual of serious play, of cosmic proportions.

There would be an exchange of symbols—of words and images, of shell and crystal, of bread and wine, of ring and triangle, of gold and silver, of earth and water, of fire and air . . .

At it, all creation would be represented. The guests of honor would be our non-human friends. We are waiting to hear from them about a suitable date . . . What follows is one outline of the marriage rite.

The Setting

Let the music of the spheres be our wedding song
and the flowers of the world our bouquet.
Let our Mother the Earth be our altar
and the sky our cathedral roof.
We are proud to have the trees and the mountains

the seas and the animals, the fish and the birds
as the witnesses of our marriage
at this holy hour.
We, N and N, are the loving consciousness of the universe
we are the human concentration of the love of creation
and when we become one this moment
EVERYTHING does.
Because we are the symbol of the planets
the sacrament of the cosmos.

The Call

We are called by the scattered fragments
into one piece.
We are called by all that is unfinished
into a new completion.
We are called by all that is separate
into a new whole.
We are called by the discords of life
into a new harmony.

The Revelation

In this moment of love is revealed
—the secret of God
—the light within the darkness
—the shape of the mystery
—the destiny of all creation
—the reason for everything
—the triumph of truth
—the stuff of heaven

The Paradox

We are old   We are young
We are ugly   We are beautiful

We are white   We are black
We are male   We are female
We are nothing We are everything
We are empty   We are full
We are silence   We are sound
We are noise   We are music
We are apart   We are together
We are mind   We are heart
We are body   We are spirit
We are One   We are Three
We are Four   We are Seven
We are every heart that ever loved
We are every life that ever lived
We are   everything

The Declaration

I love you with wonder at the mystery that you are
because you are as mysterious as God in your power

I love you with trust in the pain, the silence,
the emptiness and the darkness of our womb
where we will birth a fragile but eternal beauty;
therefore with my body I thee worship

I love you with a passion that establishes creative
breakthrough
and cosmic birthing as the condition of our lives

I love you with a hunger for the justice, peace and
compassion
that our marriage will achieve
in the transformation of the earth

Therefore when I hold you
I hold the world
when I touch you

I touch the universe
when I kiss you
I kiss the stars
when we make love
the earth is quiet
when we sleep together
the planets are smiling
when we play together
the spheres are dancing
when we are in pain
the gods are weeping
when we are in ecstasy
the cosmos reels

The Invocation

In the name of the North and the South,
the East and the West
In the name of the Earth and the Wind
the Fire and the Water
In the name of the Summer, the Winter
the Spring and the Fall
In the name of all human and non-human life
In the name of the first Fireball
and the last star
In the name of the Love
that is God . . . .
I MARRY YOU

The Exchange of Vows

I vow to set you free TO BE—
by the power of our love
I vow to bestow upon you, the gift of yourself—
by the power of our love

I vow to die to my fear of losing you—
by the power of our love
I vow to live now only that you may grow—
by the power of our love
I vow to love you, my love, with a love always new—
by the power of our love.

NOTES

1. Sam Keen, *The Passionate Life* (San Francisco: Harper and Row, 1983) p. 192.

2. Ibid. p. 204.

3. Matthew Fox, *Meditations with Meister Eckhart* (Santa Fe: Bear and Co., 1983) p. 15.

4. Phyllis Trible, *God and the Rhetoric of Sexuality* (Philadelphia: Fortress Press, 1978) p. 144.

5. Bernard of Clairvaux, *On the Love of God* (London: Mowbray and Co., 1950) p. 72.

6. Sue Woodruff, *Meditations with Mechtild of Magdeburg* (Santa Fe: Bear and Co., 1982) p. 46.

7. Richard Southern, *Western Society and the Church in the Middle Ages* (London: Penguin, 1979 reprint) p. 326.

8. Ibid. p. 327.

9. Fox, pp. 29, 28.

10. Caroline Bynum, *Studies in the Spiritualities of the High Middle Ages* (Berkeley and Los Angeles: University of California Press, 1982) p. 46.

11. A. Norman Jeffares, *Yeats: Selected Prose* (London: Macmillan and Co., 1974) p. 87.

12. Sally McFague, *Models of God* (Philadelphia: Fortress Press, 1987) p. 130.

13. Ibid.

14. Keen, p. 247.

15. Ibid. p. 252.

16. Teilhard de Chardin, *Le Milieu Divin* (London: Collins, 1960) p. 59.

17. Keen, p. 255.

18. Thomas McDonnell, *A Thomas Merton Reader* (New York: Doubleday/Image, 1974) p. 434.

19. Keen, p. 201.

20. Ibid. p. 231.

21. Brian Swimme, *The Universe Is a Green Dragon* (Santa Fe: Bear and Co., 1984) p. 45.

AUGUST

The Teaching Heart

A writer arrived at the monastery
to write a book about the Master.
"People say you are a genius.
Are you?" he asked.
"You might say so," said the
Master, none too modestly.
"And what makes one a genius?"
"The ability to recognize."
"Recognize what?"
"The butterfly in a caterpillar;
the eagle in an egg; the saint
in a selfish human being."
—ANTHONY DE MELLO

There must always be two kinds of art: escape art, for man needs escape
as he needs food and deep sleep; and parable art, the art which shall
teach man to unlearn hatred and learn love.

—W. H. AUDEN

The Teaching Heart

Much as I enjoyed giving the talks and lectures I really got high on the applause afterward. My friends would point out that this applause was not as long or as loud as I somehow seemed to imagine! But for me it was music. And I worked hard to make it happen in many cities and over many years. My preparation absorbed me in fitting and priming words and sentences for maximum explosive power on impact. I loved the words and I would select them with infinite care. I wanted to be known as a "wordsmith." Piece by piece—the humorous, the personal, the evocative—I would build up a talkful of content, ready mixed to the last detail, and irrespective of the context of the audience, the routine would be played out. There will, I realize, always be a place for formal "input" in education, but in recent years another model of teaching and learning is gradually evolving and with new power. (I use the word "teaching" deliberately. The proud tradition of this word has become devalued during the past decade or two and in this final section of the book I wish to reclaim for it some of its former dignity.)

Creative Education as Making Space

The shift in my understanding of what education meant was radical. By way of preparation, for instance, instead of filling my head with more knowledge to off-load into other more empty heads, I now tried to empty my heart of what it already knows so as to prepare it to be filled with the rich experiences of others. The content shifted from a body of spiritual insight to the insight of spiritual bodies as the community setting drew forth the wisdom already within.

> Man can be taught perhaps only
> That which he already knows,
> For only in the soul that is ready
> Grows the mind's obstinate rose;
> The right word at the wrong time
> Is wind-caught, blown away;
> And the most that the ages' sages'
> Wisdom and wit can say,
> Is no more to the quickest pupil
> Than a mid-wife's delicate steady
> Fingers aiding and easing
> The thought half-born already.[1]

In this transformation of education a new dynamic was birthed. My role was now to facilitate the opening of each heart to reveal its own beauty with confidence, in the company of other soul-friends. It seemed to me that what was now important was a quality of stillness and a condition of sensitive listening. If the "new" context of learning and sharing is to develop, then these characteristics must be cherished by the teacher. (I use the word "teacher" since I assume a similar transformation in the notion of "teacher" and "student" as we are working toward in the concept of education itself.) I refer to a need for space—space for feelings and space for silence. Fear of feelings can make the prospect of emotional space frightening. Knowing her own fears only too well, the honest teacher or guide or facilitator will realize that most students, young and old, share similar anxieties about exposing ignorance, about making mistakes before peers, about being challenged in public, about losing self-esteem. The teacher's suppressed emotion about her role, her "authority,",her acceptance by the group, her degree of democracy and respect for individual freedom and opinion, often at the expense of timely decision-making, her need for affirmation and for a sense of belonging—all these will cause frustration and impatience that eliminate any true learning in the course of its gestation. Submerged feelings undermine education. Students are students and they are not teachers. It is up to the teacher to establish the space to which I refer—a space where it is safe for feeling to emerge because the teacher has already blessed it by placing at its center her own vulnerability. In this way the power of the emotions are enlisted in the search, rather than in controlling it. This respect for, and education of, the emotions is of far-reaching importance. Since truth is the ultimate teacher here, and the educational setting is simply the setting-up of the space by teacher and students for a mutual reaching toward the truth, or rather for a mutual readiness to be grasped by it, the provision of emotional space is essential: because we can meet truth only in our wholeness and also, because our feelings are very often a surer guide to what is truthful, in their power of assimilation, integration and connection-making ability, while an unbalanced cognitive approach often turns out to be overly detached in its critiquing and analyzing.

To be vulnerable with a sense of security. To expose one's emotions, perhaps for the first time, and not be damaged. To trust the community spirit and to be right in doing so. There can be no room for carelessness here. I have been present on occasions where some kind of mutual presence went very astray and students felt cheated, cheapened and "invaded" in their first and fearful risking of revealing very personal feelings. In many situations the hurt is temporary and the healing can follow, but not always. One can only prepare oneself more thoroughly for the sensitivity of the challenge and privilege of this kind of human growth. One way of enriching the experience of sharing, and obviating to some extent the possibility of such an occurrence of trampled emotions, is the preparation of another "space." This is closely linked to, and leads to, and grows from, the space for feelings just discussed. It is the space for silence. Where "free speech" is the rule at the model of education in question, I have seen words used (and I have made my contribution) as a cloud to confuse, as a barrier to protect, as a weapon to hurt, as a slogan to preach, as a banner to impress and as packing to fill a sudden silence. In The Silent Heart we explored some of the positive aspects of silence. It was essential to the desert teachers. "If our speech is to become more truthful it must emerge from and be corrected by the silence that is its source." Silence is not failure, and progress must not be measured by noise. Silence, when introduced carefully, is a potent force for learning. It opens the heart-space essential for the emergence of wisdom. It halts the hard, fast, flying tumble of raveled and jumbled words that only distract and often intimidate. In recent sessions I have seen students react in sudden frustration. One, accustomed to the Quaker model of education, tearfully expressed her frustration at the random directions of fast-paced exchanges between fluent talkers where nobody benefited very much. Another, covering her ears, sobbed, "Stop it; stop it please . . . those words, words, words." For an interesting reflection on this issue, including a reference to the Quaker practice of "the clearness committee" (above) I refer the reader to Parker J. Palmer's book *To Know as We Are Known: A Spirituality of Education* (San Francisco: Harper and Row, 1983), from which the following extract is taken:

Sometimes I use a simple rule that allows silence to occur naturally instead of requiring my intervention. I merely ask a student not to speak more than twice (or three times in an emergency) in the course of an hour's conversation. The results are quite remarkable. Because of the pauses, many more people speak during the slowed pace than in the normal free-for-all discussion. The quieter, more retiring students suddenly find the space to speak. They also find a new responsibility to speak. . . . Often I discover that students who say little in fast-paced conversations have gifts of deep insight—perhaps because they have been forced to spend most of their lives in quietly thinking things over (p. 80).

The aim is that all concerned should deepen their humanity; that through fostering creativity a new sense of self would emerge; that a more vibrant sense of life would be the justification of the education process; that imagination should be incarnated in creative expression. The power explodes when through the media of the creative arts, hearts are put in touch with each other and with the underlying cosmic love that is the source of all things new and that sustains the universe. Michelangelo wrote:

> Sculpture, the first of arts, delights a taste still
> strong and sound: each act, each limb, each bone
> are given life and lo!, man's body is raised.
> Breathing alive in wax or clay or stone.
> But oh, if time's inclement rage should waste, or maim
> the statue that man builds alone
> its beauty still remains, and can be traced back to
> the source that claims it as its own.[2]

But so often we have judgmental attitudes toward our own self-expression. This is the result of unrelenting criticism by others as we grew up—for not meeting the expectations of parents, the examination standards of the school system and the dualistic requirements of many preachers. Pablo Casals asks,

When will we teach children what they are? We should say to each of them: do you know what you are? You are a marvel. You are unique. In all the years that have passed, there has never been another child like you. And look at your body—what a wonder it is! Your legs, your arms, your clever fingers, the way you move. You may become a Shakespeare, a Michelangelo, a Beethoven. You have the capacity for anything. Yes, you are a marvel. . . .[3]

That we are created in God's image is a truth to be assimilated slowly. It is wondrous to believe that we are living co-creators of divine beauty, blessed with extraordinary power and grace. It is to be filled with reverence, gratitude and joy. It is to see all creation as Love's Body. "Seeing yourself as a blessing is to have a healthy sense of self-esteem—which is what our world keeps from the poor and the oppressed. Self-contempt is what they reap from the oppression they internalize, which keeps them powerless."[4]

To nourish, affirm and establish the royal personhood of all people is no easy task. In fact this may be the most challenging generation of all in which to accomplish this transformation. That is why every learning experience should offer opportunities to freely play with, explore, shape and make new creations in a number of art forms.

We are all born artists; born to act and play, whether building sand castles, touching the strings of an instrument, or making ravioli. We all have the potential but are in many ways impeded from furthering it—primarily because negligence and non-participation, passive spectatorship, and therefore boredom and violence all belong to the same circuitry.[5]

Learning by Subtraction

Recently a group of us were exploring ways of growing in awareness and of being creative in a variety of forms. I was still surprised that so many encountered barriers either to the body movements suggested in our guided meditation, or to the practical sessions with clay and paint afterward. The words "distrust," "fear," "resistance," "shadow," "inability" were all mentioned. I too was feeling vulnerable in my unaccustomed role but can only agree with Matthew Fox regarding the source of these barriers.

. . . it should be emphasized that art as meditation presumes, as all of creation spirituality does, trust. A trust that out of silence, waiting, openness, emptiness one can and will give birth to images. The facilitator in such a prayerful exercise must believe deeply and therefore trust each individual present to be capable of birthing his or her own symbols or images or pictures. Such a leader allows silence to be silence. . . . More of this leaving or letting be is needed in worship and education if the people of our society are to come to shared truth.[6]

The reader will have noticed that we have reflected on these dark forces within us throughout the book. Noticed, too, will be the double-sided grace—trust and letting go—that transcends and transforms those negativities into creativity. We need to have a divine obsession with trusting ourselves, our spiritual bodies, each other, the world, all life, the cosmos itself—the Body of God. And then the letting go begins to happen and creativity flows. This letting go is an extraordinary experience that may have to be practiced as often as we trust our hearts and lungs to keep us alive. I do not mean that the process of "letting go" is a useful tool for successful education. I mean that once "letting go" is the fundamental condition of our lives, then everything to which we are truly present will be a constant realization of blessing and creative greening surpassing our wildest imagination.

Henri Nouwen compares resistance to learning with a

deeper resistance to conversion, calling for a "kenotic" self-encounter.

We will only be able to be creatively receptive and break through the imprisoning strings of academic conformity when we squarely face our fundamental human condition and fully experience it as the foundation of all learning . . . teacher and student are both sharing the same reality, naked, powerless, destined to die, and, in the final analysis, totally alone and unable to save each other. . . . Only if they are willing to face this painful reality can they free themselves for real learning. For only in the depths of loneliness, when one has nothing to lose anymore and does not cling any longer to life as an inalienable property, can one become sensitive to what really is happening in the world inside, and be able to approach it without fear.[7]

It is at this intense high point of consciousness that creativity explodes into existence; this is the anvil on which new shapes are forged. "Beauty is born of the coupling of love of life and its harmonies, with pain at life and its discords," writes Matthew Fox, and goes on to remind us of the words of the creation-centered mystic Mechtild of Magdeburg about this dialectic.[8] Each day we drink from two cups—one with red wine, one with white. The red wine symbolizes pain, suffering and loss; the white represents bliss, harmony and ecstasy. They both mingle within us and wisdom comes to be. Wisdom, always compassionate, grows from within and is nurtured by the heart; knowledge, when not laced with love, comes from outside and lodges in the head.

> Knowledge and wisdom, far from being one,
> Have oft-times no connexion. Knowledge dwells
> In heads replete with thoughts of other men;
> Wisdom in minds attentive to their own.
> Knowledge a rude unprofitable mass,

The mere materials with which wisdom builds,
Till smooth'd and squar'd and fitted to its place,
Does but encumber whom it seems t'enrich.
Knowledge is proud that he has learn'd so much;
Wisdom is humble that he knows no more.[9]

Knowledge can never be the justification for education; because knowledge as possession only increases fear. The person who knows how to split the atom but who is without the wisdom of the heart is a terrifying threat to the world.

True intelligence and wisdom reside in learning how to observe and how to listen, how to really attend to the spiritual depths of oneself, of one's neighbor and of the cosmos itself. There is a call to openness and to sensitivity. Paolo Freire's education for "critical consciousness" and Gabriel Moran's understanding of education as "resistance to closure" seem to reflect many of these values.[10]

Education and Transformation

I leave the last words in this section and in the book itself to two prophets of their times and for ours, Meister Eckhart of the fourteenth century and Krishnamurti of the twentieth. With them we pick up and further develop the issues already introduced—the nurturing of inner creativity, the growth of wisdom and trust through the letting go of resistance and fear, the transcending of the conventional but inadequate model of education. Krishnamurti claims that the current educational method can never provide the impulse for social change because it does not see the central task as being the transformation of the individual or the community. Education, as we have it, does not empower people with personal responsibility or self-esteem, but primes them to take their place in a society where violence, oppression, militarism, consumerism, inequality and prejudice are considered to be the norm. This form of indoctrination smothers spontaneity and creativity, tames a healthy discontent and ultimately nurtures fear. It aims at comfort, security and conformity as the individualistic values by which power, success and status are ensured and authentic challenge is reduced to a minimum. "This fear of life, this fear of struggle and of new experience, kills in us the spirit of risk and transformation."[11]

We develop a conditioned subservience to authority in its various shapes and forms—including governments and organized religion (which Krishnamurti refers to as "the frozen thought of man, out of which he builds temples and churches")—and lose our primordial sense of attention to the inner promptings of our deep and divine lives. We begin with an ideology, a doctrine, a tradition and seek to establish its authority in the eyes of others. We discourage and suspect creativity, doubt, difference, disagreement, and in the process damage people's capacity for relationship. "There is no existence without relationship; and without self-knowledge all relationship with the one and with the many, brings conflict and sorrow."[12]

There is something of immense importance for our spiritual growth here. So much of genuine education has to do with connecting. For me, so much of my vision has clarified itself by a regular transcendence today of yesterday's new integration. Like a reverse kind of cosmic camera zoom one realizes, as one creates space and freedom, interconnecting and revisioning, that the mystery is infinitely holistic and that loving consciousness of open relationship is at the heart of true vision.

How can anyone be compassionate toward her neighbour who is not compassionate toward herself? . . . Since friendly relations with another spring from friendly relations with yourself. Moreover I advise you to let your own "being you" sink away and melt into God's "being God" . . . and you will come to know his changeless existence. . . .[13]

To be set in context in this way; to know yourself as the heart of the body and apprehend the veins and arteries as part of yourself; to be the story-teller of your own history—this is the dynamic setting, the educational milieu, for the river of creativity and spiritual flow. A somewhat similar desire in the 1960s was typified in the "Roots" phenomenon; today the story has an earlier beginning and a later ending. "The idea that we are 'star stuff' is not a poetic fancy but a literal statement describing the birth of the elements of which we are composed in the primeval fireball from which all matter took form."[14] Amazing transformations are happening to those of us who are just discovering the story of our birth, infancy and adulthood as outlined in the earlier sections.

Matthew Fox suggests that this fact of our inter-penetration is so overwhelming that it may explain why we have erected boundaries and categories that assure us of our autonomy, among which are nationalism, racism, sexism, and religious sectarianism.[15] There are echoes here of Krishnamurti's comments about the conventional education of children: "We seek to fulfill ourselves in our children, to perpetuate ourselves through them. We build walls around them by our beliefs and ideologies, fears and hopes—and then we cry and pray when they are killed and maimed in wars, or otherwise made to suffer by the experiences of the life we have fashioned."[16] These barriers and walls are built with the bricks of our inattention to the wholeness of each person and to the place of each person in the wider whole. Our preoccupation with the linear scale of past, present and future results in three corresponding dominant concerns—the authority of remembered traditions, the authority of immediate knowledge and the authority of projected ideals. The person's worth is therefore measured against the manner in which one fits into the prevailing tradition, the knowledge that must be learned and the kind of person who would be expected to result from such training. But this is precisely how fear is made. Krishnamurti argues that while we may escape back into our traditions, forward into our ideals and outward into our inherited present,

. . . we can never escape fear by this means. For freedom from fear can only arise when boundaries are penetrated and self is integrated by its own authority.

We have come to a point in history where we have to create a new culture, a totally different kind of existence, not based on consumerism, militarism and industrialization, but a culture based upon a real quality of religion. Now, how does one bring about, through education, a mind that is entirely different, a mind that is not greedy, not envious? How does one create a mind that is not ambitious, that is extraordinarily active and efficient, that has a real perception of what is true in daily life? . . . Find out. Listen to everything, to the birds, to that cow calling. Learn about everything in yourself, because if you learn from yourself about yourself, then you will not be a second-hand human being! We like to repeat and follow what other people prepare because it is the easiest way to live. We now have to find out what it means never to conform and what it means to live without fear. This is your life and nobody is going to teach you, no book, no guru, no god. You have to learn from yourself. It is an endless thing, it is a fascinating thing, and when you learn about yourself from yourself, out of that learning comes wisdom.[17]

The radical task of education, therefore, is to help people to *discover themselves;* for to transform the world there must be regeneration within ourselves. "Where shall we begin?" asks the Meister. "Begin with the heart." Indeed Eckhart had already blazed this educational trail many centuries ago but the world did not follow the path. He preached about being still and learning from nature the meaning of the mystery. "Every single creature is full of God and is a book about God. Every creature is a word of God. If I spent enough time with the tiniest creature—even a caterpillar—I would never have to prepare a sermon. So full of God is every creature."[18] And regarding the quest for self-knowledge (the key, for Krishnamurti, to becoming wise) Eckhart repeats one of his greatest contributions to the process of spiritual growth, "If a cask is to contain wine (wisdom) you must first pour out the water (fear). For the person who has learned letting go and letting be no creature can any longer hinder. . . ."[19]

As we come to the end of these reflections, let us return for the last time to the power of fear. Fear, and fear alone, is the blasted tyranny that must be transformed. It is fear, we are assured, that lies at the root of all sin and crime. How do we avoid building another barrier to keep it out, another wall to protect ourselves? Or how do we engage it, overcome it and dismantle its powerful structures? In the context of education it has to be transcended and transformed rather than vanquished and banished. Its energy has to be enlisted and absorbed rather than channeled away in another direction. Because there is not another direction for fear. In "The Dark Heart" we reflected on the creative power of the "owned daimon" within us when harnessed and constructively ordered. So too, perhaps, with fear. It provides the tension and pressure that makes growing possible. There is a sense in which, without it, courage and freedom would not be quite as we now experience them. In education for creativity we are living through a power struggle when the almost unsuppressible power to break through engages with the almost unshakable resistance to the unknown. We feel it in ourselves every day; we sense it in others all the time. The learning shift is, in fact, accompanied by a variety of emotions, all of which contribute to creative stress and they range across a continuum: uneasiness, excitement, confusion, anxiety and fear. This tension is described in *The Teachings of Don Juan* by Carlos Castaneda:

He slowly begins to learn, bit by bit at first, then in big chunks. And his thoughts soon clash. What he learns is never what he pictured, or imagined, and so he begins to be afraid. Learning is never what one expects. Every step of learning is a new task, and the fear the man is experiencing begins to mount mercilessly, unyieldingly. His purpose has become a battlefield. . . . He must not run away. He must defy his fear and in spite of it he must take the next step in learning, and the next, and the next. He must be fully afraid and yet he must not stop.

The true teacher must be willing to let go, to be wrong, to allow the learner another reality because God only knows what wars in the soul explode into fury when trembling adult fingers close, for the first time perhaps, around a small piece of common clay. Teaching has suddenly become a sacred, awesome, and humbling privilege for the disciplined and prepared heart. But the risk brings rich rewards for the teacher and learner, insofar as they can be distinguished.

. . . the exhilaration of breakthrough, of getting to the other side, the relief of a conflict healed, the clarity when a paradox dissolves. Whoever teaches us this is the agent of our liberation. Eventually we know deeply that the other side of fear is a freedom. We must take charge of the journey, urging ourselves past our own reluctance, confusion and fear to new freedom. . . . And somewhere, always, will be that clear memory of the process of transformation: dark to light, lost to found, broken to seamless, chaos to clarity, fear to transcendence.[20]

Education is about preparation to enter and survive in the graceland of fearful beauty that most of us miss forever. If we are lucky (or is "lucky" the word for the experience of the wound inflicted by those special glimpses of terrible allurement?) we become free enough to realize that because of some strange and dark power we are held in prison and in this prison we know we are not meant to be. And the ache will not go away. It gives no peace. Something calls and beckons. It is always smiling, always promising. It is full of love. It is, I sometimes think . . . but oh, up ahead, and at the turning, I dimly see a face and form. It is, I'm sure, my cosmic child, waiting for me to join her.

* * *

And so, my faithful reader, thank you for coming this far with me. Without you I could not have kept going. As you may have guessed by now, I am an apprentice-pilgrim in this holy land. You may set out on your own one of these days. If you do, you will need a map to negotiate the landscape of the new countryside. This will be my gift to you. It is precious and perfect—but you must learn to read it well. It is, in fact, already your best friend and it beats inside you. Its rhythm will tell you all you need to know. "I am certain of nothing," wrote the poet John Keats to his friend Benjamin Bailey, "but the holiness of the heart's affections and the truth of the imagination—what the imagination seizes as beauty must be truth, whether it existed before or not." Where then shall we begin? Begin with the heart.

NOTES

1. Violet Madge, *Children in Search of Meaning* (London: SCM Press, 1965) p. 102. Quoted in O'Leary and Sallnow, *Love and Meaning in Religious Education* (Oxford: U.P., 1982) p. 79.

2. Joseph Tuisiani (trans.), *The Complete Poems of Michelangelo* (London: Peter Owen Ltd., 1961) p. 77, No. 85. Quoted in O'Leary

(ed.), *Religious Education and Young Adults* (London: St. Paul Pub., 1983) p. 45.

3. Pablo Casals, *Joys and Sorrows,* quoted in *Educating for a Global Future* (Global Education Associates, 1987) Vol. 8, No. 3–4, p. 49.

4. Joann McAllister and Matthew Fox, "Creation Spirituality: Education and Essence," quoted in *Educating for a Global Future* (Global Education Associates, 1987) Vol. 8, No. 3-4, p. 53.

5. Eric Wesselow, *Making or Breaking: Art as Education,* ibid. p. 39.

6. Matthew Fox, *Original Blessing* (Santa Fe: Bear and Co., 1983) p. 193.

7. Henri Nouwen, *Creative Ministry* (New York: Doubleday and Co., 1983) pp. 18–19. Quoted in O'Leary (ed.) (1983) p. 82.

8. Fox (1983) p. 213.

9. William Cowper, "A Winter Walk at Noon: Bk. VI," in *The Poetic Works of William Cowper* (Oxford: U.P., 1934). Quoted in O'Leary and Sallnow (1982) p. 115.

10. Theresa Sallnow, "Krishnamurti and Education: A Prophet for our Time," in *New Review* (1986) Vol. 4 No. 3 p. 32.

11. Jiddu Krishnamurti, *Education and the Significance of Life* (London: Victor Gollancz, 1978) p. 10.

12. Ibid. p. 38.

13. Matthew Fox, *Meditations with Meister Eckhart* (Santa Fe: Bear and Co., 1983) pp. 105 and 46.

14. Fox and McAllister, p. 454.

15. Ibid.

16. Krishnamurti, p. 28.

17. Jiddu Krishnamurti, *On Education* (London: Orient Longman, 1974) p. 14.

18. Fox (*Meditations . . . * 1983) p. 14.

19. Ibid. p., 54.

20. Marylin Ferguson, *The Aquarian Conspiracy: Personal and Social Transformation in the 1980's* (London: Paladin, Granada Pub., 1982) p. 322.

HEART-SCHOOL

Brief Study-Guide
Suggestions
for Director/Facilitator
of Work-Shops/Retreats

૨૦

Since this book grew, in part, from interaction with groups, it offers a basis for exploring creation-spirituality with others. Group-leaders will be familiar with techniques and strategies for preparing programs, for facilitating initial introductions and subsequent non-threatening sharing, for developing the skills of creative listening and sensitive input, thus providing a climate of openness and emotional space. Trust will grow, making room for "letting go," and healing will then happen. (I have reflected at some length on these issues in The Teaching Heart.)

I wish now to recommend a further twofold dimension of shared growth and spiritual empowerment. While familiar to many, the experience of *guided meditation* may need some explanation for most. It is a most effective and dynamic way of getting in touch with the sources within, and perhaps this is why, almost always, a significant resistance to the risk involved in such a venture can be detected.

Most of us are capable, in some sort of way, of guiding the meditation of others, but it requires skill, imagination and a prayerful loving heart to set others free to trust in their unique powers and to communicate with their own inner selves through imagery and heart-thinking. This freedom is a basic human condition available to all who set their hearts on pursuing the struggle to win it, and the gifted director will discern the appropriate approaches toward the regenerating of such life-forces. In the meantime, manuals abound with ideas and examples of activities, visual media, appropriate music and exciting imagery to help those who are attracted to guided meditative prayer.

As well as guided meditation, I have found the experience of art-as-meditation particularly moving and quite exciting in its effect on participating members. This exercise can be best described as a mode of extrovert self-expression which brings art and spirituality together in a creative form. This is usually achieved through dancing, clay-work, painting, music, drama, story-telling or massage. The experience of such centering is based on a trust that out of the initial apprehension leading to emptiness and openness, birth will be given to healing images.

It may be important to remember that we are always beginners in this non-competitive exercise called art-as-meditation, always finding ourselves and losing ourselves at the same time. While providing the appropriate guidance, setting and materials eventually becomes second nature to the director through practice and perseverance, it is only through personal and intimate communion with the four seasons of the heart that one is graced with the blessing of inspiring confidence in frightened adult seekers and thus continuing with the transformation of the universe by spreading a new spirituality for lovers.

What follows are some suggestions around which guided

imagery, personal sharing and art-as-meditation may be woven, as a study-group works its way through the book. The following pages contain only examples of how its many reflections can become the setting (or starting-point) for a program of prayer and study, based on my particular understanding of creation-spirituality as presented in each "month" of *Year of the Heart*. It is, however, important to remember that while a transformation of heart, and therefore of micro-cosmos, is never easily won, requiring a commitment to a policy of unending "letting go," all growth in prophetic vision is ultimately the pure and gracious gift of Love herself.

THE AWAKENING HEART

Autumn · September

"You have read that we are God's seed; that we will grow into God as a pear seed grows into a pear tree and a hazel seed grows into a hazel tree." After some discussion of this or a similar statement from the above section, a time of quiet would be appropriate for reflection to deepen the awareness of this amazing truth. The quest here is to discover the pattern of holy destiny in our lives, the recurring but usually hidden evidence of the "divine indwelling" in our most intimate selves. If guided meditation seems suitable, some images may be suggested to get people started. For instance, the sun will always make its presence felt no matter how persistent the clouds; the perennial grass will grow again no matter how long the drought; the winter may be empty, long and dark but the phenomenon of spring is already and always stirring within. In a comfortable space, unhurried and secure, the seeking heart will awaken to the relentless flow of the underground river that waters the equally persistent condition of dryness that threatens our joy. What is attempted during this time of reflection is to acknowledge the moments of blessing that grace our days and to realize that these privileged visitations are none other than the surfacing into our consciousness of the deeper current of God's greening power that never goes dry. "If you entrust yourself to the river of life," Krishnamurti promises, "the river of life has an astonishing way of taking care of you."

The theme of "awakening" is rich in possibilities where art-as-meditation is concerned. The awakening of the body to its own deep mystery and beauty is often accomplished by meditative massage. The grace of "letting go" so that God can be God within us is facilitated by spontaneous movement or free dance. Likewise with the medium of clay or paint. For those unfamiliar with the experience of art-as-meditation it is important for the leader to allay all anxiety (which will almost certainly be felt at the beginning) by explaining the purpose of the exercise and by emphasizing each person's potential for this kind of creativity in a non-comparative setting. I have learned that it is impossible to overestimate the fear of, and resistance to, letting go in our very vulnerable hearts.

THE WONDERING HEART

Autumn · October

Psychologists elaborate on "peak moments" and "disclosure-points" in our experiences. Our hearts are graced with primal vision as the blinds are withdrawn and fugitive beauty, for a moment, mysteriously floods our spirit. Guided meditation into such special moments of deep awareness from the past or present—moments of overwhelming wholeness, of profound bliss, of mystical unity—will often recapture vignettes of the original vision. Subsequent sharing of such lasting impressions from childhood or adulthood, with relevant details of time and place, persons, colors and moods, will be not only deeply moving but radically healing as well. It is a blessing, one of God's extravagant graces, when the gift of wonder is once again bestowed on one of us; when we are granted the vision to see what happens as new and full of music. This is the quality of the abundant life that readers of *Year of the Heart* desire to make their own.

Art-as-meditation, through prose, poetry or painting, will then further energize participators, or initiate the process, by calling forth again the pristine apprehension of reality accorded, at the beginning, to all Love's children. This calling forth will gradually provide a readiness for many more glimpses, through the windows of wonder, into the love and meaning at the heart of all creation, the small and simple as well as the great and famous.

THE COSMIC HEART

Autumn · November

The participants will have read the relevant section of the book. It is an amazing story. Because of recent scientific insight into the mystery of creation it can be called one of the greatest (and latest) stories ever told. In guided meditation the extraordinary journey of our cosmic conception, pregnancy and birth may be retraveled in imagination. Facilitators will devise their own imagery in words and audio-visuals to do justice to these almost incredible revelations.

Without infringing on individual freedom of fantasy I tend to offer a focus or theme for clearer glimpses of the unfolding mystery: that humanity is discovering itself to be the self-consciousness of evolution, that we are the world awakening to its own beauty, that God has become incarnate in us bestowing an immense responsibility to care for his body the Earth. It is good news that Christianity, along with other mainstream religions, is recovering its sense of our cosmic origins and responsibilities. Art-as-meditation provides the context for telling and, in a sense, for becoming this riveting story through the medium of the creative arts. There is a universal kind of dying and rising, a constant central love, a guiding power, an ever-present threat of total annihilation, an urgent call to responsibility, and a need to trust in God. As participants explore with paint and clay their inner feelings and voices, a more profound understanding of the sequences of transformation and of moments of incarnation in their own lives will emerge. Reflection on the breakthroughs and destiny of the universe sheds liberating light on our personal growth. It becomes clear that there is only one story. The common spirituality at the heart of the cosmic and the personal is revealed, for the Christian, in the most mysterious tale about the awesome creator of the wheeling galaxies who became a baby in one of them—in our world, and not so long ago. To forget the words of this narrative about the Word itself, the primordial storyteller, is to hopelessly lose our way. Not only are we the stuff of the stars, we are the heart of God.

The eternal Word has taken upon himself our earthy condition
giving our human nature immortal value.
So enchanting is this communion between Love and humanity
that in Christ the world bestows upon itself the gift of Love's own life.

    (Christmas Preface III: The Roman Missal)—my translation.

THE SILENT HEART

Winter · December

Recently a group of us explored this theme during a two-hour evening session. A candle flickered in the middle as we reflected on the experience of silence and darkness. These, we felt, were powerful elements and were connected with the struggle to "let go" so that we could find empty spaces in our hearts. "Letting go," we discovered, as we quietly shared our images and thoughts, is unusually difficult. We quickly sensed the prejudices, biases and judgmental attitudes that prevent us from being objective and fully present to what is happening in our lives. We spoke about the seductive power over us of knowledge, the clinging to security, the attraction of conformity and the consequent dependence and anxiety. In guided meditation we explored a number of ways to empty ourselves of preoccupation with the past and apprehension about the future. Their stifling control must be broken in our dying to self so that life can be lived freely in "the now." Staying with the present and letting go of the rest is both exhilarating and frightening.

The candle provided sufficient light for us to work with the clay which we had already prepared for the unfamiliar hands of our guests. (As teachers, Suzanne—my mentor—and I tried to stay sensitive to the strange resistance within humans in the face of new experiences of learning. That is why I wrote earlier that "God only knows what wars in the soul explode into fury when trembling fingers close, for the first time perhaps, around a small piece of common clay.") Once we were satisfied with the shapes and forms we had slowly created as we went with our feelings that evening, we suggested that we might let go of what we had made by changing it and transforming it into another shape, another creation of our spirit. Some participants found this exercise intensely difficult. They wished to hold on to this object of beauty, this child of their own heart-life, in a somewhat desperate fashion. The transformation exercise was repeated and we ultimately felt that we had befriended a very powerful and ambiguous dimension of our magnificent human nature.

THE DARK HEART

Winter · January

Not all is well with our hearts. They are complex and mysterious worlds. Sometimes they seem to possess an independent and powerful life of their own, now bright, now dark. "Within every heart bide angels and devils." In guided meditation we are carefully encouraged to visit some of the unlit corners of our psyches, to identify and then to encounter our strange shadow-force that is as ubiquitous as the light itself. As readers may know, the intention is not to destroy this dark counter-power within because, in some mysterious way, the wrestling with the demon of resistance sets up a dynamic tension for creativity and growth. With competent guidance, and after a spirit of trust within the group and in the leader has been established, we set off in imagination through the doors of the decades, to relive some of the moments when our capacity for evil seemed so shocking. "We aim to strike back when we are hurt, to get even when we are let down, to destroy and even to kill in the face of infidelity, betrayal or ridicule." With free movement, to suitable music, in a dim light, in response to guided imagery, within a small group and with a professional presence, the beginnings of genuinely enriching and liberating experiences can happen.

The owning and expression of such twilight encounters can often be achieved through art-as-meditation sessions. Writing is particularly helpful in facing up to the existence of suppressed forces denied during, and since, the days of childhood. That such unhealthy spiritual squatters be identified, healed and then befriended in time is of the greatest importance. Left to fester and decay in the unexamined cellars of our psyches, these powerful drives will surely poison and finally totally destroy our delicate but resilient spirit. (Many of my questing friends have relied on journaling and dream analysis as an exciting and satisfying way to safely reach a level of integration and inner-connectedness, bringing with it a new empowerment and another harvest of spiritual growth.)

THE WOUNDED HEART

Winter · February

This session has to do with issues of profound sensitivity. The usual careful preparation is made through relaxation, comfortable position and breathing, letting go of distractions, awareness of one's inner self. One very delicate area that needs skillful guidance is the world of memories and ever-present feelings of rejection in the past or present, in the classroom, socially or at home. Sometimes deeply-buried hurt will emerge from the graves of the past when careless intolerance, ridicule and rejection left their festering wounds. "You can't do it. Don't try." "You're telling lies. No one will believe you." "Don't be a stupid and lazy dreamer. You'll never get anywhere." "You silly child. Don't you really fancy yourself!" (The list here is as varied as the group.) Allow time for the perception of the effects of such thoughtless exchanges—the weakening of the self-image, the erosion of confidence, the helpless but raging sense of injustice in the face of false accusation, the long-term hurt caused by the shock of betrayal.

A rereading of The Wounded Heart will provide many areas for fruitful but fragile exploration. May I emphasize again how sensitive this journey back in time is and how traumatic it can be when one encounters in fantasy, one of the people who inflicted some of the scars that never healed. It is essential for tutors and leaders to have a great respect for the ambiguous powers that are ready to explode in such private pilgrimages. Surrounded by love and very gradually, and maybe at a later time than this session, some of the bitterness that has poisoned the spirit, some of the cold spell that has frozen spontaneous creativity, will begin to lose power, and a new love, energy and freedom begins to emerge. (In many instances where there is severe psychic injury, skilled professional help will be required.)

THE YOUNG HEART

Spring · March

We try to enliven once again within our adult hearts some of the qualities of childhood that we reflected upon earlier in the book. These characteristics of the divine are many and beautiful—trust, openness, vulnerability, a sense of play, of living in "the now," an awareness of the immediate and a capacity for letting go. Of particular relevance in guided imaginative prayer is the gradual sensing of the original childhood delight in moments of immediacy, spontaneity and full commitment to the present moment. Because the work-ethic of our culture has become second nature to many of us, this aspect of our hidden child has faded over the decades, and much patience is required in our attempts to live again in fantasy, in that carefree land. Work often becomes an avenue of escape from facing the reality of our true feelings. For reasons that we examined in The Wounded Heart, instead of letting our emotions be fully felt within us, we become progressively alienated from our feelings and we bury them alive. This is the beginning of the death of our first and only child.

The guided meditation is to nurture this child back to life, by reliving and experiencing again in memory, occasions of trust, loving response, immediate joy, carefree play, and a readiness for adventure. It is exciting to hold a conversation with your child who, initially, will be weak and shy, but who, with comforting, nourishment and much loving, will grow strong and vibrant to become the life-giving play-mate of your soul. In this prayer-time that heals the memories, the first sharing will be about recalling the hidden stories of suppressed emotion—buried feelings of hostility, sexuality, anger and outraged justice. The strengthening effect of these liberating encounters provides the confidence for trusting in life and love again, leading to a slow letting-go that heals even as it hurts. Thus does the journey begin. The imagery, the stories and the appropriate art-as-meditation will provide the nourishment and the milieu for the health of our divine child on whose vibrant growth the abundant life depends.

THE GREEN HEART

Spring · April

This chapter in the book is simply a version of my life-story up to now, told in the imagery of a stained-glass window. I have drawn on symbols such as the sun, the ivy, the child, to express some of the dominant forces throughout the decades and passages of the years. The idea came to me suddenly and the various dimensions of the story fell into place readily. At this session the opportunity for telling each one's life-story might be provided. The telling could include all or any of the creative modes of expression we have often referred to. Because each person's story is unique, just as every creative effort is, there is no comparing or set standards. The only guideline is to be true to the inner self. For all the vicissitudes of life with the turns and twists of destiny to emerge in each one's story, much "letting-go" and trusting is necessary. A certain kind of control must be set aside and left-brain domination must make room for right-brain celebration. The experience and the fruits of it will be intensely fulfilling.

It is often recommended that a time of guided meditation would precede the "activity" of organizing the communicable expression of the personal journey. An alternative symbol could be explored as a chart for such a unique exploration. The imagery of a river is always a powerful and rich one. It has dimensions of variety, of twists and turns, trials and errors, fixity and fluidity, stillness and turbulence, continuity and flexibility, individuality yet a shared essence with the waters of the world. The story of a tree, the coming of a slow dawn, the regular metamorphoses of nature with which we are familiar—all of these and many more can allure us into the space where life-giving revelations about who we truly are emerge into our consciousness. During the same session or at a later date, through free clay-work or painting, for instance, such moments can be gradually focused, intensified and eventually multiplied.

THE CREATIVE HEART

Spring · May

Eric Gill reminds us that while every artist may not be a special kind of person, every person is a special kind of artist. Most of us realize that we actualize only a tiny part of our creative potential, our immense inner resources. How do we activate the sleeping power within our unconscious? What divine kiss will awaken the royal artist reclining deep within? We must learn the language of imagery. We therefore need to practice using our imagination—"thinking with our hearts" instead of calculating with our minds always.

Here is one way to bring to the surface the creativity that springs at our center. (Prepare in the usual way for guided imagery through relaxation, etc.)

"Imagine a well . . .
the old-fashioned kind . . .
with a little shingled roof,
and an oaken bucket hanging from a rope . . .
and a handle, to raise and lower the bucket.
Look at the well from a distance.
Imagine the landscape—the setting of the well.
Slowly . . . leisurely . . . picture the surroundings
(Elaborate on these).
Notice the season of the year.
    Feel the warmth or coolness of the air.
    Smell the air.

Now draw close to the well.
  Stand beside it and touch it.
  Feel the coolness and strength of the stone sides . . .
    the texture of the wooden parts . . .
    the smoothness of the handle . . .
    its resistance to being turned . . .
    the weight of the bucket . . .
    the roughness of its wood . . .
Look into the depths of the well.
Feel the coolness rising from the depths.
Smell the freshness of the pure, clear spring water in the well.
And know that you are very like the well.
  You have at your depths a wellspring
    of clear, cool water . . .
    an unlimited source of wisdom . . . creativity . . .
    strength . . . power . . . goodness.
  You have the ability to draw up
    from your innermost depths
    that great untapped energy . . .
    to bring to the light of your consciousness
      your own inner resources . . .
    and to drink your fill . . .
      to satisfy the thirsting of your parched soul . . .
    and to share your rich gift with all those
    whose lives you touch . . .
    and to sing and dance for joy
    to celebrate life in its fullness.
And to know that you have met your God within.

Jean Gill, in *Images of Myself* (Paulist Press, 1982), offers this meditation (pp. 5–12) to set us on our way toward our creative inner self—the well-spring of imagination and power. We can regard the bucket in the above imagery as our capacity for symbolism, a readiness for fantasy. Let the link between the conscious and the unconscious, or perhaps the communication between the left brain and the right brain, be signified by the rope. The particular image used may be a tree, a river, a moving cloud. The picture is complete when we understand the handle that lowers and lifts the bucket as the activity, technique or exercise that charts our course into the rich unconscious and guides us to the dark waters where birthing happens. It is from this still womb-well that the transformation begins.

THE EUCHARISTIC HEART

Summer · June

In this session we try to reclaim the richness of sacramentality and symbolism. Celebration of the Eucharist is concerned with more than personal fulfillment. Personal healing is part of universal healing. The hunger after justice and peace where the poor live nourishes our own poverty. In guided meditation we move imaginatively from the broken body of Christ to the needy group of believers who gather to remember and honor that death. On the table, at the center, are some pieces of bread and some poured-out wine. Like a cosmic astronaut, try to see in these symbols a ravaged, bleeding and dying Earth where the wonders of creation are looted and polluted. See, for the moment, the plight of people. Let the images multiply. Watch yourself comforting those in deep despair, almost insane with loss and grief. Feel the pain of the "anawim"—the neglected and despised of our society. Feel the pain of the universe, the animals, the trees, the seas, the air, the top-soil. As we absorb some of the cosmic crucifixion we identify with the suffering figure on the Cross but also with the redeeming power of the same redeeming love. In some mysterious way, by taking on ourselves the slow destruction of our beautiful planet and its amazing people, we become identified too with its re-creation and salvation. We return in imagination to the Eucharistic gathering where we trust that our open and broken hearts are large enough to receive and then to heal the whole world, the Body of God.

The challenges to the reader in this section may seem extreme. Art-as-meditation will offer opportunities to enter into a new grasp of symbolic and sacramental realities. Just as the wedding-band symbolizes worlds of pain and passion in one tiny circle, so too with broken bread and spilled wine. In dance or touch, in word or clay, in paint or drama, the attempt is made to encapsulate the dimensions of nature and humanity, the past, present and future, that are caught up in the elements of the Eucharistic celebration. Participants could be encouraged to write their reflections, a personal kind of Eucharistic Prayer, where their own life-story as well as that of the universe, is traced in the rich symbolism of the bread and wine. Small groups could take one dimension each in dance or story such as "memory" or "interconnectedness" or "mourning" or "hope." A final presentation during a Eucharistic celebration might open new windows into the ever-present mystery.

THE EROTIC HEART

Summer · July

Readers of *Year of the Heart* will notice the theme of blessing and celebration running through the seasons. Currently misused and misapplied words like "pleasurable" and "erotic" are being recalled from the shadows of mistrust into which they had been pushed by a belief-system and set of values that had become excessively fearful. They, among many other such terms, had a proud and beautiful history in the service of God and redeemed humanity before being poisoned by Jansenistic dualism and sold into pornographic slavery. Scriptural references to God's ecstasy and his sheer delight and pleasure in creation and Incarnation are once again coming center-stage before a long-deprived audience. The reclaimed and purified terms are applied as the eroticism of creativity is once again being celebrated for the divine blessing that it is. Almost every creative experience can be erotically satisfying. And so too with human sexuality. It is a beautiful, spiritual and powerful God-given human condition that permeates all our lives. Once this reality is suppressed our spirituality becomes severely distorted, because human sexuality is a reflection of God's own nature. It is one way of expressing to another the depths of divine passion.

In *Prayer That Heals Our Emotions* (Contemplative Books, 1986), Eddie Ensley writes about how the marriage embrace can become a prayer. This is another way of speaking about art-as-meditation and about a spirituality for lovers.

(Prayerful sex is) an attitude of open loving presence to one another that allows God's love to flow in you and through you. . . . When you come together, begin first by sharing your feelings and your emotions. If you have anger or resentment toward your spouse, get that out. Take time to ask forgiveness and forgive one another for any ways you might have hurt each other. Be sure to share positive, uplifting thoughts and feelings about each other since you last shared. Such sharing of the goodness you see in one another is a way of loving each other into wholeness. . . . Take time now for silent meditative prayer. . . . You will be amazed at what a loving awareness you have of the other person in this quiet time of preparation. . . .

With the tenderness of your touch express the tenderness of God. And when you are caressed and touched, receive that not only as the love of your spouse, receive it with the same reverence as you would the caress of God in the bosom of your soul (pp. 93–95).

In making love lovingly, I suggested earlier in The Erotic Heart, divine Love itself is intimately at play in a moment which symbolizes both intense personal passion and awesome cosmic attraction. Something uniquely precious to God is repeatedly incarnated everytime that the act of love is appropriately celebrated. And just as in the becoming flesh of divine love in Jesus Christ there was transfiguration, loneliness and vulnerability unto death, so, too, in the loving embrace there are echoes of ecstasy, the "little death," and, strangely, intimations of a deeper longing.

THE TEACHING HEART

Summer · August

Among the issues raised in this section of the book are education as drawing out rather than putting in, emotional space and reflection-space in the sharing sessions, the power of vulnerability, liberating the imagination, the suspension of judgment, encouraging creativity, the centrality of unlearning, the fear of letting go, the resistance to learning, and transformation through compassion. The spirituality for lovers which is at the heart of this book is not best served by the current principles of formal education. We search for a paradigm shift away from an institutionalized, often threatening and almost violent kind of teaching and study where knowledge is pursued as possession for power, to a more loving, playful and trusting sharing in the compassion and wisdom of the community.

The "content" of The Teaching Heart is really concerned with a strategy for communicating hearts, when mystery whispers to mystery across the chasms of the spirit (rather than a teaching topic in itself as with the other sections). Nevertheless the creative reader will be waiting for a challenge. And here it is. How would you set about selecting an urgent issue from the material in this last section and shaping it for sharing with a small group of adults? How would you prepare for this? How would you bring your own heart and those of others to a condition of readiness? Have you ideas about the best place, the light, the furniture, the temperature, amount of input, the aim of the session, the introduction, the exact role you give yourself, the issue of silence and emotional space, difficulties with participation and incompatible personalities?

How will you know if it's successful?

And where will you begin?

Begin with the heart.

Bibliography

Alves, Ruben. *Tomorrow's Child*. New York: Harper and Row, 1972.

Armstrong, Edward. *Saint Francis: Nature Mystic*. Los Angeles: University of California Press, 1973.

Balasuriya, Tissa. *The Eucharist and Human Liberation*. New York: Orbis, 1979.

Boff, Leonardo. *St. Francis: A Model for Human Liberation*. New York: Crossroad, 1984.

Brewi, Janice and Anne Brennan. *Celebrate Mid-Life*. New York: Crossroad, 1988.

Bynum, Caroline. *Studies in the Spiritualities of the High Middle Ages*. Berkeley and Los Angeles: University of California Press, 1982.

de Chardin, Teilhard. *The Phenomenon of Man*. New York: Harper and Row, 1959.

———. *Le Milieu Divin*. London: Collins, 1960.

———. *Hymn of the Universe*. New York: Harper and Row, 1969.

de Mello, Anthony. *One Minute Wisdom*. New York: Doubleday, 1986.

Davies, Paul. *God and the New Physics*. New York: Simon and Schuster, 1983.

Deloria, Vine. *God Is Red*. New York: Dell Publishing Co., 1973.

Edwards, Denis. *Human Experience of God*. New York: Paulist Press, 1984.

Ferguson, Marilyn. *The Aquarian Conspiracy*. California: J. P. Tarcher, 1981.

Fox, Matthew. *Meditations with Meister Eckhart*. Santa Fe: Bear and Co., 1983.

_____. *A Spirituality Named Compassion*. San Francisco: Harper and Row, 1979.

_____. *Original Blessing*. Santa Fe: Bear and Co., 1983.

_____. *Breakthrough*. New York: Image Books 1980.

Fox, Matthew and Brian Swimme. *Manifesto for a Global Civilization*. Santa Fe: Bear and Co., 1982.

Frager, Sheikh Ragip. *Love Is the Wine*. New York: Threshold Books, 1987.

Griffiths, Bede. *Return to the Center*. Illinois: Templegate, 1976.

Hammarskjöld, Dag. *Markings*. New York: Knopf, 1964.

Harman, Willis and Howard Rheingold. *Higher Creativity*. Los Angeles: Jeremy P. Tarcher, 1986.

Harnan, Nicholas. "A Spirituality of the Heart." *New Review*, Vol. 2, No. 1, p. 32.

Hoffman, Bob. *No One Is To Blame*. Palo Alto, CA: Dutton and Co., 1979.

Hopkins, Gerard Manley. *Collected Poems of Gerard Manley Hopkins*. New York: Oxford University Press, 1967.

Jacobi, Jolandi. *Masks of the Soul*. London: Darton, Longman and Todd, 1976.

Jones, Alan. *Soul Making*. New York: Harper and Row, 1985.

Jyoti, Amar Swami. *Retreat into Eternity*. Boulder, CO: Gold Hill Publishing, 1981.

Keen, Sam. *The Passionate Life*. San Francisco: Harper and Row, 1983.

Kelsey, Morton. *Christo-Psychology*. New York: Crossroad, 1988.

Kennedy, Eugene. *A Time for Love*. New York: Image Books, 1972.

Krishnamurti, Jiddu. *On Education*. London: Orient Longman, 1974.

_____. *Education and the Significance of Life*. New York: Harper and Row, 1981.

Lonergan, Anne and Caroline Richards, ed. *Thomas Berry and the New Cosmology*. Mystic, CT: Twenty-Third Publications, 1987.

Lutyens, Mary, ed. *Krishnamurti's Journal*. New York: Harper and Row, 1982.

Madge, Violet. *Children in Search of Meaning*. London: SCM Press, 1965.

McAfee Brown, Robert. *Spirituality and Liberation*. Philadelphia: Westminster Press, 1988.

McCarthy, Flor. *And the Master Answered*. Indiana: Ave Maria Press, 1985.

McDonagh, Sean. *To Care for the Earth*. Santa Fe: Bear and Co., 1987.

McDonnell, Thomas. *A Thomas Merton Reader*. New York: Image, 1974.

McFague, Sally. *Models of God*. Philadelphia: Fortress Press, 1987.

McNeill, Donald, Douglas Morrison and Henri Nouwen. *Compassion*. New York: Image Books, 1983.

Miller, Alice. *The Drama of the Gifted Child*. New York: Basic Books, 1981.

Miller, William. *Make Friends with Your Shadow*. Minneapolis: Augsburg, 1981.

Mische, Patricia. *Star Wars and the State of Our Souls*. Minneapolis: Winston Press, 1985.

Murchie, Guy. *The Seven Mysteries of Life*. Boston: Houghton Mifflin Co., 1978.

Neihardt, John. *Black Elk Speaks*. New York: Washington Square Press, 1932.

Nouwen, Henri. *Creative Ministry*. New York: Doubleday, 1971.

O'Collins, Gerald. *The Second Journey*. New York: Paulist Press, 1978.

O'Leary, Donal and Theresa Sallnow. *Love and Meaning in Religious Education*. Oxford: O.U.P., 1982.

———. *Religious Education and Young Adults*. London: St. Paul Press, 1984.

Palmer, Parker J. *To Know as We Are Known*. San Francisco: Harper and Row, 1983.

Pearce, Padraig. *Plays, Stories, Poems*. New Hampshire: Longwood Publishing Group, 1980.

Peck, Scott. *The Road Less Travelled*. New York: Simon and Schuster, 1980.

_____. *People of the Lie*. New York: Simon and Schuster, 1983.

Potter, Dennis. *Son of Man*. London: Penguin, 1971.

Rahner, Karl. *Theological Investigations IV*. New York: Crossroad, 1974.

_____. *The Eternal Yes*. New Jersey: Dimension Books, 1964.

_____. *Hearers of the Word*. London: Sheed and Ward, 1969.

Robbins, Lois. *Waking Up in the Age of Creativity*. Santa Fe: Bear and Co., 1981.

Robinson, Edward. *The Original Vision*. New York: Harper and Row, 1983.

Shmemann, Alexander. *The World as Sacrament*. New York: St. Vladimir's Press, 1974.

Sinetar, Marsha. *Do What You Love: The Money Will Follow*. New York: Paulist Press, 1987.

Smith, Cyprian. *The Way of Paradox*. New York: Paulist Press, 1987.

Soelle, Dorothy. *The Strength of the Weak*. Philadelphia: The Westminster Press, 1984.

Solignac, Pierre. *The Christian Neurosis*. New York: Crossroad, 1982.

Southern, Richard. *Western Society and the Church in the Middle Ages*. New York: Penguin, 1979.

Steiner, Rudolf. *The Kingdom of Childhood*. New York: Rudolf Steiner Press, 1964.

Swimme, Brian. *The Universe Is a Green Dragon*. Santa Fe: Bear and Co., 1984.

Teselle, Sallie. *Speaking in Parables*. Pennsylvania: Fortress, 1975.

Uhlein, Gabriele. *Meditations with Hildegard of Bingen*. Santa Fe: Bear and Co., 1985.

Vanstone, Howard. *The Stature of Waiting*. New York: Harper and Row, 1983.

Walker, Alice. *The Color Purple*. New York: Washington Square Press, 1982.

Woodruff, Sue. *Meditations with Mechtild of Magdeburg*. Santa Fe: Bear and Co., 1982.

Yockey, James Francis. *Meditations with Nicholas of Cusa*. Santa Fe: Bear and Co., 1987.